Just Pretend!

Creating Dramatic Play Centers with Young Children

Written by

Judy Nyberg

Illustrated by

Cyd Moore

GoodYearBooks
An Imprint of ScottForesman
A Division of HarperCollinsPublishers

GoodYearBooks

are available for most basic curriculum subjects plus many enrichment areas. For more GoodYearBooks, contact your local bookseller or educational dealer. For a complete catalog with information about other GoodYearBooks, please write:

GoodYearBooks

ScottForesman

1900 East Lake Avenue

Glenview, IL 60025

Design by Lynne Grenier.

Copyright © 1994 Good Year Books.

All Rights Reserved.

Printed in the United States of America.

ISBN 0-673-36116-0

1 2 3 4 5 6 7 8 9 — MH — 02 01 00 99 98 97 96 95 94

C O N T E N T S

CREATING DRAMATIC PLAY CENTERS WITH YOUNG CHILDREN

From *Just Pretend!* by Judy Nyberg. Copyright © 1994 GoodYearBooks.

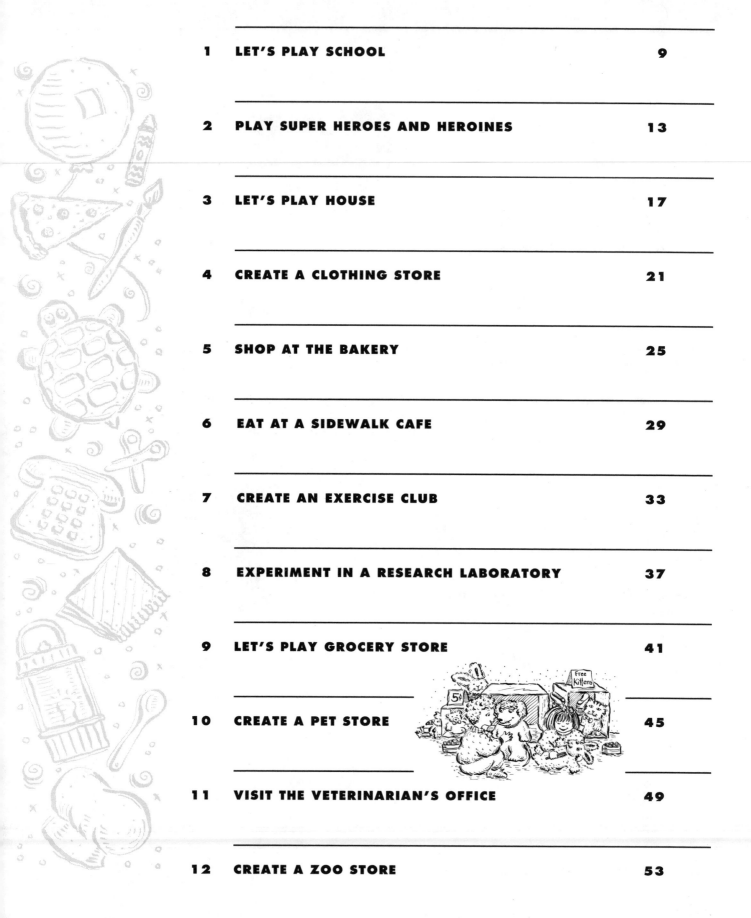

Creating Dramatic Play Centers with Young Children

The Importance of Dramatic Play

The chicken is in the oven; the vegetables are on the stove. The table is set with tablecloth and flowers. Mom is wearing her gorgeous flowered dress and newest high heels. Dad has chosen to wear a boldly striped tie and a green apron. He is concerned about the choice of vegetables. The blue and yellow plastic pegs will taste better than the jewelry that is now cooking. Mom is reluctant to change the menu. She thinks the plastic pegs will taste fine. Mom and Dad argue briefly. Fortunately, the dinner guests arrive without announcement and the argumentative hosts graciously welcome them with good manners.

As teachers and observers of young children, we have often seen similar scenes unfold as children engage in sociodramatic play. The play can be surprising, filled with unexpected twists, interruptions, and resolutions. It is sometimes exuberant, angry, noisy, or messy. It is always purposeful and meaningful to the participants. Dramatic play opportunities should not be limited to preschool and kindergarten children, but should be enjoyed in all primary classrooms. Dramatic play activities are especially appropriate for after school programs and summer programs.

Learning Through Play

The importance of play in the development of young children has long been understood and supported by early childhood specialists. Experts in this field have tried to convince the rest of the educational world not only that play is valuable, but that it also should have an honored place in the curriculum throughout the primary grades.

The learning that takes place during dramatic, or symbolic, play has been acknowledged by Piaget, Vygotsky, and other teachers of early learning theories. Through play, children assimilate new information and consolidate it with past experience. It is also believed that play stimulates symbolic, abstract levels of thought. Dramatic play gives children opportunities to experiment with and interact with objects and ideas. They construct their own learning and meaning as they manipulate objects, make connections to past experience and hear new language.

Purposeful dramatic play, reflecting content being taught in the curriculum, becomes the ideal integrated activity as children incorporate art, science, social studies, language, small and large muscle skills. That's why dramatic play opportunities should not be limited to preschool and kindergarten children, but should be enjoyed in all primary classrooms. These activities are clearly appropriate for after school programs and summer programs, too.

Pretending to Be Someone Else

When children pretend or role-play, they often try on the behaviors of the adult world. "Mom" and "Dad" disagree about appropriate vegetables but they do know how to refrain from their discussion in the presence of guests. The doctor prescribes, the teacher gives homework, the truck driver makes everyone get out of the way, and the sales person persuades the customer to buy. When role-playing, children practice functional, meaning-filled roles as they imitate behaviors and conversation. Children use new vocabulary and concepts, carry out action plans by planning the sequence of events and problem solve in their own sociodramatic play.

Socialization During Play

Children learn to negotiate during play. They learn to take turns, to give and take control, to share, and to be fair. If they deviate from these sophisticated social conventions, they quickly learn the consequences inflicted by their peers. Children gain self confidence when allowed to play and interact with others. They rejoice because play allows children to feel that they are in control of situations. They use play to enhance relationships with friends and to discover how friendships work. They exert their newly-found powers of bargaining and persuasion, and solve their own problems. Play allows children to express feelings. Play feels good.

Literacy Development and Play

Recent research has shown that dramatic play promotes cognitive development in general and literacy development in particular. Dramatic play provides opportunities for children to practice functional literacy activities, such as reading and writing, and to exhibit literacy-related behaviors, such as using story language or the language of books. When children retell stories through story reenactment, they more readily conceptualize the story. When they try on character roles, they learn about characters' feelings, events, and story sequence. They use the language of stories in their play, a basic pre/beginning reading skill. When children become Goldilocks or one of the three bears, the story becomes their own. When they become the Big Bad Wolf, they utilize all of their new-found knowledge about how they think wolves behave in stories. They apply new concepts to their play.

Developing Oral Language

The use of oral language is inherent in dramatic play as children converse and role-play with one another. The conventions of conversation are tried on. Questions are posed and answered, turn-taking is necessary when talking, and tone of voice reflects emotions and feelings. Along with conversational language, children expand vocabulary as they interact in play. All children have specific or limited background experiences on which they base their vocabularies and understandings. When exposed to books and to language models in the home and classroom, concepts and vocabulary are expanded. When engaged in dramatic play, children have opportunities to "try on" or "actualize" those concepts and vocabularies that they have not previously experienced. After listening to and watching teacher models of conversation and literacy behaviors, children will incorporate literacy events in their dramatic play.

Writing and Reading During Play

An emergent literacy perspective supports the belief that children learn to read and write by engaging in real reading and writing and by being immersed in a print-rich environment. Dramatic play provides opportunities for children to engage in functional literacy activities and to practice literacy-related behaviors. Their play can be based on models they see every day. Some children see family members reading at home. Moms and dads read newspapers, phone books, cookbooks, directions, billboards, and maps. They see people reading signs while shopping at stores, going to movies, and in museums. Children also watch adults write grocery lists, letters, and messages. They watch as people in the adult world write checks, fill out forms and applications, and order from catalogs.

Resources in *Just Pretend!*

Dramatic play centers can become exciting print-rich areas where children realize the importance and functions of reading and writing activities. *Just Pretend!* contains a listing of literacy-related materials that can be included in each of its 24 suggested dramatic play centers. These are the same kinds of materials that children see adults using in real life. In addition, a blackline master is provided for each center, containing from 1 to 3 forms modeled after those that adults might actually use. All of these adult-like forms encourage children's writing as they play.

As you introduce a new center, talk with children about the literacy materials that you have included. Look together at the catalogs, pamphlets, signs, charts, books, etc., and discuss how they are used and why they are important. Read the forms with children and, as you talk about the information that could be written on them, model how to fill them out.

Encourage children to practice with the forms in the center. Assure them that they can write as they are able, using real, "pretend," or even scribble writing. The intent in these activities is to give children opportunities to practice with functional forms—to see the reasons why people write. Children are not expected to write conventionally or to necessarily read the forms on their own.

A listing of picture books related to the theme of each dramatic play center is included, too. Reading with children before the center is established and during its use will enhance their understanding of the focused concepts. You will also want to place these books within each center for children to read and explore for themselves.

The "housekeeping corner" or "home-living center" has become a tradition in most preschool programs. This center, typically equipped with stove, refrigerator, table and chairs, is often the setting for most spontaneous dramatic play. While dramatic play equipment is usually evident in most kindergarten classrooms, the furniture is sometimes turned toward the wall, to be used only with permission and on occasion. Sometimes the dramatic play center is neglected—filled with tired, worn materials that invite neglect. In classrooms beyond kindergarten, dramatic play centers are not usually even evident.

Perhaps dramatic play spaces would flourish throughout the primary grades if there were a universal understanding among educators and parents that dramatic play is not synonymous with "housekeeping corner," but rather an opportunity for a myriad of possible settings where wonderful imaginings and learning take place.

Your classroom may already have a dramatic play area. However, if you do not have the luxury of a designated spot with permanent props such as child-sized furniture, dress-up clothes, etc., you can still establish an area for dramatic play. Rearrange the classroom furniture and equipment you do have to clear a corner or other suitable space. Create "prop boxes" that contain clothing and materials necessary to develop a specific theme, such as a grocery store, weather station or camp site. Creating various "prop boxes" can become a shared project: the boxes can rotate throughout several classrooms.

Dramatic play areas should be provided outside the classroom, too; child care centers, after-school programs and summer programs for school-age children provide ideal settings. The centers become excellent arenas to develop themes—pioneer days or space exploration, for example. School-age children will delight in the opportunity to contribute props and activities to dramatic play areas over a sustained period of time.

Teachers know that the energy, enthusiasm, and excitement they model when a new topic or idea is introduced motivates children's response and involvement. After introducing the focus for each center by reading books, showing real objects and pictures, and sharing conversation, invite children to determine with you how the new center should look, where it should be located, and the materials and props that should be included. Encourage children to make their own materials and costumes. When the center is established, demonstrate literacy events, such as how appointments or reservations are made on the phone, and how reading materials, such as maps, magazines, or recipes are used. Model the conversations that salespersons, research scientists, or museum guides would use in real life. Remember that the teacher's major function is to provide ample time, space, and equipment for play.

Teachers can be aware of their children's individual needs as they play in socio-dramatic settings. Often, children need teacher interaction to get play started. Some children need an invitation or encouragement to become involved in the play. Others need teachers to briefly involve themselves in the play, acting as a guest at a restaurant or a client in the health club.

Teachers can model language and behaviors while remembering that the play belongs to the children and should not be taken over by the teacher or adult. We can disengage ourselves from the play when our role as facilitator is no longer needed.

Involving Parents

Parents are often a rich source for providing props and objects needed to create dramatic play centers. A parent in the food service industry can provide menus, brochures, hats or food containers. A banker can supply deposit slips, receipt books, computer print outs, envelopes, and coin rolls. Parents are happy to supply baby bibs, rattles, diapers, and blankets. Notify parents before setting up a center and enlist their help in gathering supplies. Encourage parents to visit the classroom as guest speakers when a dramatic play center is related to their work or hobbies.

All teachers have their own levels of tolerance for noise, mess, and activity. Does it bother you when children bring manipulatives, blocks, or dishes from one center to another? Do loud voices and play wrestling create tension for you? Do galloping horses and frontier clashes make you anxious? Be aware of your levels of tolerance as you set guidelines for play.

1. Establish clear rules for the use of the center, such as limiting the number of children in the center at one time.

2. Demonstrate how equipment is to be used and be consistent in supervising appropriate use.

3. Write simple rules for the center on a poster so that children can refer to them when they play.

4. If equipment is misused, remove it or limit its use.

5. The amount of materials in the center greatly affects order or contributes to chaos. Children are much more interested in playing in a center that is organized than in one that is messy.

6. Label boxes or containers, such as *jewelry, shoes, scarves, plastic animals,* and *play money,* so that children can put materials away independently.

7. Give children sufficient warning when play is about to end so they can resolve situations and begin to restore order.

8. If interest in the center wanes, it's time to shut it down.

We can learn a great deal about our children as we watch them play. How do they interact with other children? Do they prefer parallel or solitary play? Are they leaders or followers? Are they often frustrated and angry? Do they manipulate their peers? What kinds of words and language do they use? Do they like to pretend and imagine? Do they retell stories in their play? Can they take turns? Choose one child at a time to observe. Write down observations over a period of time to note changes in behaviors, language, and social interaction.

The suggestions for dramatic play centers in this book demonstrate how an early childhood curriculum can be taught and extended through dramatic play. As children contribute to and play in theses environments, they reinforce concepts and vocabulary related to their expanding knowledge of the world. The concepts become a part of their own worlds and they become real. Dramatic play incorporates and integrates many areas of the curriculum. As they play, children will utilize art, language, math, cooking, science, small and large motor skills.

The centers suggested in this book are just a beginning. Some are reflections of experiences with which most children are familiar, others stimulate imagination and invention. The choice of centers should be determined by children's interests. Perhaps your children will want to create a video store, a space ship, or a baby clinic. They may want to create a fish market or a house for The Three Bears. Just pretend! Let's learn!

THE CENTERS

Let's Play School

Play Super Heroes and Heroines

Let's Play House

Create a Clothing Store

Shop at the Bakery

Eat at a Sidewalk Cafe

Create an Exercise Club

Experiment in a Research Laboratory

Let's Play Grocery Store

Create a Pet Store

Visit the Veterinarian's Office

Create a Zoo Store

Visit a Travel Agency

Work at the Office

Design an Astronaut Center

Play at a Sandy Beach

Go on a Deep-Sea Dive

Make a Classroom Aquarium

Set Up a Weather Station

Visit a Flower Shop

Let's Go Camping

Create an Insect Museum

Run a Bee Keeping Station

Explore an Underground Cave

Let's Play School

It's fun to not be yourself! That's why it's fun to play school. When playing school, a child can become a nurturing caretaker, a test-corrector, a powerful command-giver, or a mischief-making learner. Observe children's play carefully. You may see a bit of yourself.

Model Language

School play reflects the important role of school in the child's life. Kindergartners demonstrate how much they enjoy school as they assume various roles, imitating the behaviors and language of their new friends and teachers. As they grow, children's impressions of their classrooms and their own identities are revealed in their play. Children reveal their cognitive and language skills as they investigate, experiment, and initiate activities in play. Children will naturally imitate the language, vocabulary, tone of voice, and volume that you use in the classroom. Watching as they play the role of teacher can be a humbling experience. Each time a teacher speaks, he/she is providing a language model for children.

Related Vocabulary & Concepts

desk, library, chart, records, sharing, cooperation, pupil, student, homework, chalk, chalkboard, eraser, stapler

- Use topically related books, such as those in the list that follows, in introducing the center and during its use. Book-related activities should include reading aloud to children and opportunities for them to explore the books on their own.
- Designate a special area of the room where children can play school, such as a corner where a chalkboard is available.
- If appropriate, allow children to set up a pretend classroom outdoors.
- Demonstrate how to make environmental signs and labels, such as *teacher's desk* or *library*, and directional signs such as *Turn in your milk money today*.
- Provide maps, posters, or alphabet charts for display.
- Use a table as the teacher's desk.
- Provide adultlike materials that will foster literacy activities, such as chalk and chalkboard, erasers, staplers, pens, unused activity book worksheets, and books for record keeping.
- Provide book sets with records or tapes that can be used independently by children.
- Provide Blackline Master 1, *Student Record*. Talk together about why teachers keep records and how they can be used to help children. Encourage children to use the play records to practice their writing, even if it is only pretend.

School Room Equipment & Materials

table for teacher's desk	plant	2 or 3 student desks and chairs
wastebasket	posters for display	chalkboard, bulletin board
pencil sharpener	cardboard boxes for books	activity worksheets

Literacy Materials

chalkboard, bulletin board	posters	maps
writing materials, paper	notebooks	books, tapes, records
chalk, erasers	alphabet cards	individual chalkboards
stapler	Blackline Master 1, *Student Record*	

BOOKS TO READ

Duke, Kate. *The Guinea Pig ABC.* New York: Dutton, 1983. Adorable guinea pigs pose and interact with alphabet letters. (Preschool-1)

Goennel, Heidi. *Colors.* Boston: Little, Brown, 1990. A girl finds all the colors of the rainbow in familiar objects. (Preschool-1)

Hennessy, B. G. *School Days.* New York: Viking, 1990. A simple, rhyming text tells about events at school. (Preschool-1)

Johnson, Dolores. *What Will Mommy Do When I'm at School?* New York: Macmillan, 1990. An African-American girl worries about her mother as she prepares for her first day at school. (Preschool-K)

Jonas, Ann. *Color Dance.* New York: Greenwillow, 1989. Colorful dancers show what happens when colors are mixed. (Preschool-2)

MacDonald, Suse. *Alphabatics.* New York: Macmillan, 1986. Alphabet letters change shape and form and become objects that reinforce initial sound/letter relationships. (Preschool+)

Maestro, Betsy and Giulio. *Harriet Reads Signs and More Signs: A Word Concept Book.* New York: Crown, 1986. Harriet reads environmental signs as she takes a walk to Grandma's. (Preschool-1)

Martin, Bill Jr., and Archambault, John. *Chicka Chicka Boom Boom.* Ill. by Lois Ehlert. New York: Simon and Schuster, 1989. An exciting ABC with bright designs and text, inviting participation. (Gr. 2-6)

McMillan, Bruce. *Time to . . .* New York: Lothrop, Lee & Shepard, 1989. A photographic journal of a kindergartner's day that teaches the concept of time. (Preschool-2)

Schwartz, Amy. *Annabelle Swift, Kindergartner.* New York: Orchard Books, 1988. Annabelle's big sister has prepared her well for the first day of school. (Preschool-2)

Thompson, Carol. *Time.* New York: Delacorte Press, 1989. A bear has a busy day at school. (Preschool-K)

Blackline Master 1

Student Record

School Name _____

Teacher _____

Child's Name	Knows Alphabet	Date

Need to talk to parent

Notes

Play Super Heroes and Heroines

Children who are developing self-concepts and discovering the real world through their five senses often choose to engage in super hero play. Favorite super hero characters change with the times, but the reasons for young children's affection for this type of drama remain constant. Super heroes represent strength and have the potential for making powerful changes in the world. They can do what children would like to be able to do. They are protectors of the weak and doers of good. Children see these fantasy figures as positive role models.

Model Language

Invite children to talk about their favorite super heroes. Ask them to share how they know about these heroes—through television, movies, books, cartoons, and so on. Have children describe what these characters do and have them describe how they look. (Help children visualize what their heroes look like by describing your favorite hero.) Encourage children to talk about the good things that super heroes do for others or what super powers they would like their heroes to have.

Related Vocabulary & Concepts

cape, costume, power, strong, space, fly; good deeds, helping, super, protect, make-believe, magic

- Establish a space in the room where super hero drama may be enacted.
- If dress-up props are provided, make the rule that only those children dressed in the props can be involved in the play. (Teachers always have the option of keeping super heroes from entering the classroom.)
- Create the concept that super heroes can only do good things in the classroom. They do not create destruction.
- If play becomes rough or is too consuming, direct children to other activities and give the players a rest.
- Provide maps for heroes to read and paper and pencils for players to create their own maps.
- Provide Blackline Master 2, *Heroes' Secret Message Form* and *Super Hero List*. Talk together about why people use codes and why secrecy is sometimes important. Encourage children to share their codes, explain their maps, and tell others about what they have included on their Super Hero lists. (Note: The children's actual writing on these forms can be real or "pretend.")

Super Heroes Play Equipment & Materials

capes

flashlights

gloves

blocks or small empty boxes for mountains

magic power belts or headbands (aluminum foil covered)

Literacy Materials

maps

paper and pencils for secret messages and map making

super hero name signs

books or magazines for reading instructions

paper for writing secret codes

Blackline Master 2, *Heroes' Secret Message Form, Super Hero List*

BOOKS TO READ

Bond, Felicia. *Poinsettia and the Firefighters.* New York: Harper & Row, 1984. Poinsettia pig has difficulty adjusting to her own room upstairs as she deals with strange sounds and noises. The alert pig saves the day by calling the fire department. (Preschool-3)

Brown, Marc. *Arthur's Nose.* Boston: Little, Brown, 1986. By the end of this story, Arthur has learned to like his nose. (Preschool-3)

Brown, Marc and Brown, Laurene Krasny. *The Bionic Bunny Show.* Boston: Little, Brown, 1985. An ordinary bunny plays a super hero on a television show. Readers will delight in the problems he has maintaining his image. (Preschool-3)

Carlson, Nancy. *I Like Me!* New York: Viking Kestrel, 1988. Louanne Pig discovers her unique attributes. Readers will think about their own uniqueness. (Preschool-1)

Dale, Penny. *Bet You Can't.* New York: Lippincott, 1988. A brother and sister cooperate in cleaning up their rooms. Even super heroes have to clean up. (Preschool-1)

Johnson, Angela. *Do Like Kyla.* Ill. by James E. Ransome. New York: Orchard Books, 1990. A young girl tries to imitate her big sister's actions until she discovers she can do things, too. (Preschool-2)

Jonas, Ann. *Round Trip.* New York: Greenwillow, 1983. Readers will use their imaginations as they travel through this visually exciting book of images. A great book for partners to read together. (Kindergarten-3)

McPhail, David. *Lost!* Boston: Little, Brown, 1990. A fantasy about a boy who helps a lost bear find its way home to the woods. (Preschool-3)

Sendak, Maurice. *Where the Wild Things Are.* New York: Harper & Row, 1963, 1988. The classic tale of a boy who travels to an island where wild things live. (Preschool+)

Blackline Master 2

Heroes' Secret Message Form

To: _____

From: _____

Secret Code _____

_____

_____

Draw your own
adventure map.

Super Hero List

Things I need for my trip

_____

_____

_____

Good things I have done

_____

_____

_____

People I will help today

_____

_____

_____

From *Just Pretend!* by Judy Nyberg. Copyright © 1994 GoodYearBooks.

Let's Play House

When children play house, they feel a sense of control that is an essential ingredient in building self-esteem. They assume adult roles and make sense of their own identities as they act out daily living routines. Some children watch adults use literacy materials and listen to good oral language models in the home. Other children will need to see how literacy materials are used.

Model Language

Encourage children to talk about the roles family members play at home and the jobs people do there. Have children name and talk about family members. Give children daily opportunities to talk about things that have happened at home and to share anticipated family events. Discuss with children the importance of taking care of things in the home and the importance of being kind to people we love. Model telephone manners and conversation.

Related Vocabulary & Concepts

family, mother, father, sister, brother, baby, cooking, cleaning, resting, helping, caring, loving, house, rooms, furniture, household objects, cookbooks, newspapers, magazines

- Use topically related books, such as those in the list that follows, in introducing the center and during its use. Book-related activities should include reading aloud to children and opportunities for them to explore the books on their own.
- Introduce baby dolls and accessories so that children have opportunities to role-play caring for and playing with babies. Encourage children to wash, dress, feed, read to, and talk to baby dolls.
- Provide paper so that children can write grocery lists, letters, and messages.
- Provide mail to be delivered and read to one another.
- Introduce TV program guides, newspapers, and magazines. Discuss how they are used in the home and model their use.
- Children will enjoy exploring the reading materials so important in a home: cookbooks, directional manuals for installing new fixtures, and telephone books. Discuss the different functions of these and other reading materials found in the home and model how they are used.
- Maps should be available so that children can use them when they plan pretend trips.
- Writing materials, such as pads of paper and pencils should always be available in the housekeeping center.
- Provide Blackline Master 3, *Shopping List* and *Telephone Message*. In introducing the Shopping List, you may want to initiate discussion by asking children to name their favorite foods—the things they would like to buy at the grocery store. Develop a shopping list together on the chalkboard. Build understanding that lists are useful because they help us remember things that are important. Written telephone messages are useful for the same reason. (Note: Encourage children to practice their writing on these forms, whether the letters and words they use are real or imagined.)

Housekeeping Center Equipment & Materials

mirror	child-sized table and chairs	tablecloth, vase, flowers
child-sized mops, brooms	telephone	empty food boxes, cans
plastic foods	child-size rocking chair	pretend window or curtains
dress-up clothes	rug, pillows, blankets	doll bed, high chair, stroller
dishes, pans, utensils	handbags, wallets, briefcase, suitcase	
child-sized sink, refrigerator, stove, cupboard		

books	magazines	cookbooks
catalogs	maps	pencils, pens, crayons
junk mail	telephone book	different types and sizes of paper
writing materials	magnetic letters	advertisements
envelopes	Blackline Master 3, *Shopping List, Telephone Message*	

BOOKS TO READ

Aliki. *Overnight at Mary Bloom's*. New York: Greenwillow, 1987. A girl enjoys an overnight visit with a unique adult friend. (Preschool-3)

Havill, Juanita. *Jamaica's Find*. Ill. by Anne Sibley O'Brien. Boston: Houghton Mifflin, 1986. A child returns a lost stuffed animal to its owner. (Preschool-3)

Hayes, Sarah. *Eat Up, Gemma!* Ill. by Jan Ormerod. New York: Lothrop, Lee & Shepard, 1988. A brother finds something surprising for his fussy baby sister to eat. (Preschool-1)

Hines, Anna Grossnickle. *Big Like Me*. New York: Greenwillow, 1989. A big brother tells the baby what he will eventually be able to do. (Preschool+)

Hoban, Russell. *Best Friends for Frances*. Ill. by Lillian Hoban. New York: Harper & Row, 1969. Frances finds out what it means to really be a friend. (Preschool-3)

Hutchins, Pat. *The Doorbell Rang*. New York: Greenwillow, 1986. Children learn to share cookies as unexpected company arrives. (Preschool-3)

Kellogg, Steven. *Best Friends*. New York: Dial, 1986. Two friends learn that it's not always easy to resolve problems. (Preschool-3)

Komaiko, Leah. *Annie Bananie*. Ill. by Laura Cornell. New York: Harper & Row, 1987. Annie is a unique, irreplaceable friend. (Preschool-3)

Lobel, Arnold. *Frog and Toad Are Friends*. New York: Harper & Row, 1970. Five short stories about the adventures of two very good friends. (Kindergarten-3)

Marshall, James. *George and Martha Encore*. Boston: Houghton Mifflin, 1977. The hippos again prove what it means to be a friend. (Kindergarten-3)

Steptoe, John. *Baby Says*. New York: Lothrop, Lee & Shepard, 1988. A boy learns tolerance for his troublesome baby brother. (Preschool)

Blackline Master 3

Shopping List

Things I need to get at the grocery store:

_____

_____

Things I need to get at the drug store:

_____

_____

Other things I need:

_____

_____

Telephone Message

Who called? _____

What time? _____ AM _____ PM

What is the message? _____

_____

Do they want you to call back?

yes _____ no

Your name _____

From *Just Pretend!* by Judy Nyberg. Copyright © 1994 GoodYearBooks.

Create A Clothing Store

If we told children how many concepts they learn when they play store, they might not choose to play as often. They classify and sort. They learn about numbers and money. They button, tie, and take turns. And they think they are just having fun!

Model Language

Invite children to name the clothing, discount, or department stores where they shop in the neighborhood or at a mall. List the names of these stores on the board. Have children take turns talking about experiences they have had shopping at stores, describing what items they were shopping for, such as new shoes, a bed, or a toy. Explain the word *customer*. Then, have children brainstorm jobs people do in stores, such as salesclerks, stockers, and cashiers. Model dialogue that storekeepers and customers might have together by role playing a pretend visit to a store.

Related Vocabulary & Concepts

store, clothing, accessories, salesclerk, cash register, money, price tags, sale, signs, customer, bag or sack, package, catalog, sales receipt, check

- Use topically related books, such as those in the list that follows, in introducing the center and during its use. Book-related activities should include reading aloud to children and opportunities for them to explore the books on their own.
- Invite children to think of a name for a classroom store and to make signs for it.
- Have children make price tags and labels for dramatic play props to be sold, such as dresses, shirts, purses, jewelry, gloves, or shoes.
- Model for children how salespersons write sales slips or receipts; how customers write checks. Use Blackline Master 4, Sales Receipt and Check Form. Encourage children to use these forms as they practice their own writing, whether it is real or pretend.
- Provide fashion magazines, newspaper advertisements, and/or catalogs for customers to read.
- Encourage children to create store advertisements and then distribute them to classmates.
- When children play in the store, encourage them to help one another button, zip, and tie various articles of clothing.
- To facilitate organization in the store, provide labeled boxes or containers so that items can be separated and stored. All persons in the store can practice folding and organizing clothing as they create displays and return items to their appropriate places.
- Provide a mirror so that children can view themselves as they try on clothing.
- Children will enjoy moving the same items out-of-doors to create a garage or yard sale.

Clothing Store Equipment & Materials

shelves, tables	dress-up clothing	store front or puppet stage
cash register	play money	boxes for storage and display
mirror	hangers or hooks	paper bags for purchases
clothes rack	telephone	

Literacy Materials

pads of paper	checks	sales slips
price tags	pencils	fashion magazines
advertisements	telephone book	

Blackline Master 4, *Sales Receipt and Check Form*

OOKS TO READ

Berenstain, Stan and Berenstain, Jan. *The Berenstain Bears on the Job.* New York: Random House, 1987. The familiar bears get in trouble on the job. (Kindergarten-3)

Florian, Douglas. *People Working.* New York: Crowell, 1983. A simple, predictable text highlights the jobs people do. (Preschool-3)

Hest, Amy. *The Purple Coat.* Ill. by Amy Schwartz. New York: Macmillan, 1986. This is a sensitive story about a girl who needs a new coat. Her grandfather, who is a tailor, understands her wishes for a beautiful coat, not a practical one. (Kindergarten-3)

Fox, Mem. *Shoes from Grandpa.* Ill. by Patricia Mullins. New York: Orchard Books, 1990. This cumulative tale reinforces concepts about dressing and families. (Preschool-1)

McPhail, David. *Pig Pig Gets a Job.* New York: Dutton, 1990. Pig Pig learns that it's hard work to earn money. (Preschool-3)

Miller, Margaret. *Who Uses This?* New York: Greenwillow, 1990. Children are invited to predict who uses each tool that is photographed in this book. (Preschool)

Neitzel, Shirley. *The Jacket I Wear in the Snow.* New York: Greenwillow, 1989. A cumulative tale that details clothing worn when getting ready for a winter outing. Perfect for reading or chanting aloud. (Preschool+)

Spohn, Kate. *Clementine's Winter Wardrobe.* New York: Orchard Books, 1989. A book filled with detailed illustrations showing varieties of clothing. Children will enjoy identifying the articles of clothing they are familiar with. (Preschool-1)

Yektai, Niki. *Crazy Clothes.* Ill. by Sucie Stevenson. New York: Bradbury Press, 1988. Young readers will really enjoy this very silly story about clothing. (Preschool-2)

Blackline Master 4

Customer's name

Date

Total

Sales Tax

Receipt

-----✂---

The Safe Bank
500 Main Street
United States of America

Date _____ 19 _____

_____
                              Dollars
Pay
to the
Order of _____

Memo _____   Signature _____

1:3692420300 "346 448"'3" 1592

Shop at the Bakery

Patty cake, patty cake,

Baker's man,

Bake me a cake

As fast as you can.

Pat it and prick it

And mark it with B

And put it in the oven

For Baby and me.

Model Language

Lead children on an imaginary trip to a bakery shop. Pantomime walking into the store and smelling the wonderful smells. Describe the baked goods displayed in the cases: frosted doughnuts, decorated cakes, cinnamon buns, and chewy cookies. Buy a cookie and happily enjoy munching. Invite children to talk about experiences they have had going to a bakery or a pie shop.

Visit a bakery, if possible, so that children can experience the good smells and identify various products. After returning to the classroom, have children name the items they saw and list them on the chalkboard. Read *Ruth's Bake Shop* by Kate Spohn (Orchard, 1990), *This Is the Bread I Baked for Ned* by Crescent Dragonwagon (Macmillan, 1989), and *How Pizza Came to Queens* by Dayal Kaur Khalsa (Crown, 1989).

Related Vocabulary & Concepts

bakery, cake, cookie, rolls, doughnuts, breads, pie, baker, baking, shopping, smelling, looking, decorating, flavors, oven

- Use topically related books, such as those in the list that follows, in introducing the center and during its use. Book-related activities should include reading aloud to children and opportunities for them to explore the books on their own.
- Ask the school's kitchen staff if the class can visit when baked goods are being made.
- The bakery center can be set up in a corner of the classroom if other dramatic play areas are in use. Signs for the shop can be displayed and removed each day if necessary.
- Give the shop a name and involve children in making signs for the shop. Include signs that identify specials or sale items. (See Blackline Master 5.)
- Have children name their favorite kinds of real and imaginary pies. List the names on the board. Have children create their own cardboard pies to sell. Pizza pie cardboard wheels are perfect for this activity. Encourage children to make labels for their pies so that customers can see the various flavors.
- Encourage children to wear white smocks or shirts when they work in the pie shop. Provide paper so that children can make bakers' hats.
- Make a baker's apron using a white plastic tall garbage bag with a drawstring. Cut the bottom off so the bag slips over the head. Pull the drawstring at one spot to make a loop over the neck.
- Create and display recipes on charts.
- Have children create coupons, good for a free pie, to distribute to classmates.
- Demonstrate for children how to make pie slices by folding and cutting paper pies into triangular wedges.
- Use Blackline Master 5, *The Best Bake Shop Order Form* and *Today's Special.* Introduce the order form segment of the master by talking together about children's favorite bakery treats. Develop a class "Best Bake Shop Order" on the chalkboard. Encourage children to make their own lists, using real or pretend writing. For the sign segment of the master, bring in examples of actual "special" signs from your bakery or grocery store. Talk together about why bakers and other store owners use signs like these.

boxes for storage	blocks or empty boxes for display counter	
cash register	play money	cardboard pizza wheels
white shirts	bakers' hats	play oven and stove
play sink	play refrigerator	rolling pin
modeling clay	cookie sheets	spatulas
cupcake tins	cupcake liners	tall white plastic garbage bags

store signs	labels for pies	cookbooks
recipe charts	pencils, pads of paper	advertisements
coupons for pie purchase	Blackline Master 5, *Supply Order Form, Today's Special*	

BOOKS TO READ

de Paola, Tomie. *Pancakes for Breakfast.* San Diego: Harcourt, 1978. After the eggs are gathered, the cow is milked, and the butter churned, the pancakes can be made and eaten. (Preschool–2)

Dragonwagon, Crescent. *This Is the Bread I Baked for Ned.* Ill. by Isadore Seltzer. New York: Macmillan, 1989. Bold illustrations and a cumulative text show a meal being prepared for Ned who eventually shows up with lots of friends. (Kindergarten–3)

Galdone, Paul. *The Little Red Hen.* New York: Clarion, 1979. The author/illustrator tells the familiar tale in a unique way. (Preschool–2)

Hutchins, Pat. *The Doorbell Rang.* New York: Greenwillow, 1986. Chocolate chip cookies are shared as friends and neighbors drop in for visits. (Preschool–3)

Kasza, Keiko. *The Wolf's Chicken Stew.* New York: Putnam, 1987. The ending to this award-winning story surprises the wolf and readers alike. (Preschool–3)

Khalsa, Dayal Kaur. *How Pizza Came to Queens.* New York: Crown, 1989. A homesick visitor from Italy is cheered up when she can make her famous pizza. (Gr. 1+)

Morris, Ann. *Bread, Bread, Bread.* Photographs by Ken Heyman. New York: Lothrop, Lee & Shepard, 1989. This photo journal shows people all over the world baking, sharing, and eating breads. (Preschool–2)

Spohn, Kate. *Ruth's Bake Shop.* New York: Orchard Books, 1990. This picture book concentrates on baked goods and desserts. The illustrator's style is unique and inviting for individual reading. (Preschool–2)

Blackline Master 5

The Best Bake Shop

Supply Order Form

Item						Quantity	Price

Signature _____

- - - ✂ -

Today's Special

$ _____

Eat at a Sidewalk Cafe

Creating a classroom restaurant provides a wonderful opportunity to focus on children's heritages and traditions. Encourage children to contribute ideas regarding the type of restaurant to be created. Invite parents to become involved in contributing to the environment and in providing tasty treats. What are you hungry for today? Chinese? Indian? Mexican? Yum!

Model Language

Use a dramatic play area in the classroom or an outside play area to create a fast food restaurant, a restaurant that features ethnic foods, or a sidewalk cafe. Engage children in sharing the experiences they have had eating in places other than their homes. Have children name the restaurants where they have been and describe who they were with, what the restaurant looked like, and what foods they ate. Encourage them to think about the jobs that people do in a restaurant, such as cook, salad preparer, bun baker, dishwasher, floor sweeper, host or hostess, and server. If children's experiences have been limited to eating in fast food restaurants, role-play being escorted to a table by a host, reading menus, and ordering food when seated at a table. Demonstrate how servers record orders on a pad.

Related Vocabulary & Concepts

restaurant, fast food restaurant, server, waiter, waitress, hostess, customer, menu, napkin, utensils, dishes, tray, reservations, polite, manners

- Use topically related books, such as those in the list that follows, in introducing the center and during its use. Book-related activities should include reading aloud to children and opportunities for them to explore the books on their own.
- Have a "Name the Restaurant" contest, listing names on the board as children suggest them, and then vote on the name for your classroom restaurant.
- Have children make their own menus, placemats, and signs for the restaurant.
- Identify utensils, dishes, napkins, and glasses needed for place settings; have children practice setting tables.
- Celebrate cultural diversity by inviting children to talk about experiences they have had in restaurants where ethnic foods are served (for example, Ethiopian, Mexican, Italian, Vietnamese, Chinese, etc.). A parent who is familiar with foods representative of a specific culture could be invited to class to help children create menus.
- Demonstrate how to use Blackline Master 6, *Today's Special, Order Form,* and *How Was the Service?* Talk together about why each form would be important to both the customers and the restaurant workers. Then, encourage children to fill out the forms on their own, using real or pretend writing.
- Have children watch as you write a recipe on a chart so that children can make a food to be served in the restaurant.

Sidewalk Cafe Equipment & Materials

child-size table and chairs	tablecloth	napkins
dishes	table utensils	aprons
chef's hat	dress-up clothes for customers	cash register
paper flowers in vase	telephone for reservations	

Literacy Materials

order pads	pencils	menus
"table reserved" sign	"no smoking" signs	restaurant signs
"specials" signs	recipes for chef	

Blackline Master 6, *Today's Special, Order Form, How Was the Service?*

Caseley, Judith. *Grandpa's Garden Lunch.* New York: Greenwillow, 1990. After planting and caring for a garden, a child and her grandfather share a delicious vegetable garden lunch. (Preschool+)

Ehlert, Lois. *Growing Vegetable Soup.* San Diego: Harcourt, 1987. The author/illustrator's well-known graphics illustrate how vegetables are grown and later become delicious soup. (Preschool-3)

Emberley, Rebecca. *Taking a Walk Caminando.* Boston: Little, Brown, 1990. The Spanish and English text in this book identifies buildings and places in a neighborhood. (Preschool-3)

Friedman, Ina. *How My Parents Learned to Eat.* Ill. by Allen Say. New York: Houghton Mifflin, 1984. A warm story about eating customs, as told by a girl who has a Japanese mother and an American father. (Kindergarten-3)

Gross, Ruth Belov. *What's on My Plate?* Ill. by Isadore Seltzer. New York: Macmillan, 1990. A helpful concept book that tells where food comes from. Chicken comes from a chicken, of course. (Kindergarten-3)

Komaiko, Leah. *My Perfect Neighborhood.* Ill. by Barbara Westman. New York: HarperCollins, 1990. The humorous, rhyming text explains why a girl thinks her urban neighborhood is the best place to live. (Preschool-3)

Novak, Matt. *Mr. Floop's Lunch.* New York: Orchard Books, 1990. This is a tender story about a man who shares his picnic lunch with animals. (Preschool-1)

Rockwell, Anne. *Come to Town.* New York: Crowell, 1987. Readers will enjoy identifying activities that happen in familiar places in the community. (Preschool-1)

Blackline Master 6

Server	Table	Number of People

Total $

Today's Special

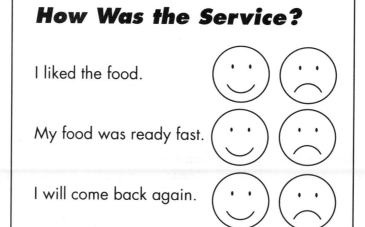

How Was the Service?

I liked the food.

My food was ready fast.

I will come back again.

Create an Exercise Club

*Do you spend time telling children to slow
down, stop running, settle down? Give them
an outlet for their natural energy and enthusiasm. Let's exercise!*

Create an Exercise Club   **33**

Model Language

Since many children have not had the experience of visiting an exercise or an athletic club, it is important to explain the concept of why people need to exercise. Talk together about the equipment people might use when exercising and the space needed to house equipment. Then, help children visualize what they might see in an exercise club. Have children brainstorm about the kinds of exercises they think people might do at an exercise club, such as running, jogging, swimming, lifting weights, and bicycling. Then, discuss the kinds of activities that could take place in and the equipment needed to create an exercise club out-of-doors on the school playground.

On the chalkboard, list activities that children could do in a gym or an exercise club, such as running, lifting weights, jumping rope, doing push-ups or leg lifts. Model the roles people play in a club and the literacy activities involved, such as taking registrations, recording client information, weighing in, answering phone calls, writing plans for individual activities.

Related Vocabulary & Concepts

exercise, club, equipment, running, jogging, swimming, healthy, shower, towels, shorts, start, finish

- Have children suggest classroom equipment that could be used, such as balls, jump ropes, bicycles, blocks to make a pretend rowing machine, a table and chairs for a registration area.
- Invite children to suggest a name for the club and to make signs.
- Provide a measuring tape and a scale for weighing-in procedures.
- Have children create advertisements for the club and award certificates for completion of courses.
- Provide a stopwatch so that children can time one another as they run or do exercises.
- Let children create, on paper, a cross-country running course for the playground, or make maps showing where running lanes could be established. Encourage children to mark the lanes and to make directional signs, such as *enter here, start*, and *finish*.
- Invite children to make diagrams of and then establish an obstacle course or fitness path.
- Provide paper so that children can make identifying numbers for runners or bikers to wear as they race.
- Use Blackline Master 7, *Client Information, Contract*, and *Fitness Plan*. Talk together about why each person should have his/her own fitness plan, emphasizing that everyone has special interests and skills—no one of us is alike. Go on to discuss why a health club would need client information and contracts. Show children how each of the forms might be filled out and then encourage them to use the forms, too, practicing with real or pretend writing.

Exercise Club Equipment & Materials

table, chairs	telephone	blocks
jump ropes	balls	bicycles
playground equipment		

34   Create an Exercise Club

paper   pencils, crayons   posters

club signs   fitness trail maps and plans   chart for recording times

Blackline Master 7, *Fitness Plan, Client Information, Contract*

OOKS TO READ

Campbell, Alison and Barton, Julie. *Are You Asleep, Rabbit?* Ill. by Gill Scriven. New York: Lothrop, Lee & Shepard, 1990. In this tender story, a little boy who is having trouble sleeping becomes concerned about his pet rabbit. (Preschool-1)

Brown, Marc. *Arthur's Eyes.* Boston: Little, Brown, 1979. Arthur is embarrassed to wear his new glasses until he learns that his teacher wears them, too. This book is a great discussion starter. (Preschool-3)

Carlson, Nancy. *Bunnies and Their Hobbies.* Minneapolis, MN: Carolrhoda, 1984. The charming bunnies in this book show that having hobbies after a hard day's work is fun and healthy. See also *Bunnies and Their Sports* (Viking, 1987). (Preschool-3)

Howard, Jane. *When I'm Sleepy.* Ill. by Lynne Cherry. New York: Dutton, 1985. In this beautiful bedtime book, a girl wonders what it would be like to sleep with animals. (Preschool-3)

Inkpen, Mick. *One Bear at Bedtime.* Boston: Little, Brown, 1987. This is a delightful bedtime counting book that will be enjoyed by beginning readers. It emphasizes that proper rest is a part of keeping fit. (Preschool-2)

Isenberg, Barbara and Jaffe, Marjorie. *Albert the Running Bear's Exercise Book.* New York: Clarion, 1984. A lovable bear is convinced that he will become a better runner if he exercises. (Preschool-4)

Blackline Master 7

Fitness Plan for

_____
Name

Monday	
Tuesday	
Wednesday	
Thursday	
Friday	
Saturday	
Sunday	

Client Information

_____
Name

_____

Address

_____

_____

Contract

I will follow the rules
of the Exercise Club
and try my best.

X _____

From *Just Pretend!* by Judy Nyberg. Copyright © 1994 GoodYearBooks.

Experiment in a Research Laboratory

Children living in the twenty-first century will experience things not yet imagined. Expand their horizons by introducing the concept of being a scientist or a researcher. Perhaps one of your children will make history!

BE SURE MICE CAGES ARE CLOSED

TURN OFF LIGHTS

KEY TO LAB

Model Language	One of children's favorite dramatic play settings is the doctor's office. Because most children have had experiences visiting a doctor's office, they play the roles of doctor, nurse, and patient with great expertise. Talk about visiting the doctor or health clinic with children, encouraging them to share procedures and experiences. Were there a lot of people waiting? Were babies crying? Did they sit on an examining table? Did children get measured and weighed? Did they go to the doctor to get a shot? How did they feel?

Introduce the concept that many doctors do not see patients in clinics or hospitals. Instead, they are scientists who work in laboratories where they study how bodies and brains, plants and animals grow; they do research on how to keep people healthy. Write the words *scientist, laboratory,* and *research* on word cards so children can refer to them as needed. Invite children to think about the kinds of activities that might take place in a research laboratory, such as making new medicines and looking at slides using microscopes. Invite children to think about why researchers would need to wear gloves as they work. (Disposable gloves can be purchased at pharmacies or hospital supply stores for minimal cost.)

Related Vocabulary & Concepts	*doctor, nurse, prescription, examination, experiment, research, scientist, microscope, germ, slide, laboratory, clean, records, files, skeleton, bones, organs*

- Use topically related books, such as those in the list that follows, in introducing the center and during its use. Book-related activities should include reading aloud to children and opportunities for them to explore the books on their own.
- Provide a microscope or magnifying glasses, tweezers, eye droppers, cotton balls, small dishes, plants, soil, shells, rocks, cloth or foods for examining. Model how microscopes are used. Show children how slides are prepared, mixing an ingredient with a small amount of water on a plastic margarine tub lid.
- Have children name the laboratory and then make signs, such as *Experiment Records, Do not touch,* and *Turn off water.*
- Children will enjoy using water for their pretend experiments. Water colored with food colorings invites mixing and experimentation. To ease clean up, have all water experiments take place in a tub or dish pan.
- Create sign-in sheets where researchers sign in and out of the laboratory and charts where they can record observations of experiments.
- Display health pamphlets that are available in doctor's offices.
- Provide picture books or encyclopedias showing anatomical illustrations for reference. Children will enjoy pictures of human skeletons.
- Encourage all researchers to wear laboratory coats (shirts or smocks). Have children make identifying badges to attach to their "coats."

- Use Blackline Master 8, *Observational Record and Data Sheet.* Explain to children that researchers can't depend on their memories. The work they do is so important that they must write down the things they are studying and what they find. Work together to fill out a sample *Observational Record* (mixing a bottle of red water with a bottle of blue water would be a good class project for this activity). Then ask children to try their hand at recording their experiments, using either real or pretend writing.

table, chairs	dish pans	microscope or magnifying glasses
plastic margarine tubs	plastic lids	tweezers
cotton balls	eye droppers	disposable gloves
test tubes	smocks/shirts	telephone

laboratory signs	health pamphlets	reference books
observational charts	sign-in sheets	pads for recording experiments
booklets for journaling	rulers	pencils

Blackline Master 8, *Observational Record and Data Sheet*

BOOKS TO READ

- Cole, Joanna. *The Magic School Bus Inside the Human Body.* Ill. by Bruce Degen. New York: Scholastic, 1989. Take a fantastic trip inside the body with Ms. Frizzle and her class. (Kindergarten-3)

- Elting, Mary. *The Human Body.* New York: Macmillan, 1986. This colorful book is a handy reference for adults that describes the characteristics and functions of the human body.

- Hutchins, Pat. *You'll Soon Grow into Them, Titch.* New York: Greenwillow, 1983. Titch always gets second-hand clothing that is too big for him. But, as the title of the book states, Titch is growing. (Kindergarten-3)

- Packard, Mary. *From Head to Toes—How Your Body Works.* Ill. by Dora Leder. New York: Julian Messner, 1985. This is a reference book that is filled with information that can be shared with young children. (Preschool+)

- Showers, Paul. Let's-Read-and-Find-Out Science Books. New York: Crowell, various dates. These books provide information and concepts about the body that young children can grasp. Titles include: *A Drop of Blood, Ears Are for Hearing, Hear Your Heart,* and *How Many Teeth?.*

Blackline Master 8

Observational Record and Data Sheet

Name of Observer _____

I am observing _____

This is what I see _____

_____

Let's Play Grocery Store

To market, to market
To buy a fat pig.
Home again, home again
Jiggety-jig.
To market, to market
To buy a fat hog.
Home again, home again
Jiggety-jog.

Because young children are familiar with the experience, playing grocery store is a popular dramatic play activity. Children especially enjoy the autonomy of being able to select their favorite items displayed in their own store. "Playing store" provides many opportunities to increase children's awareness of print as well as providing oral language experiences. Encourage children to talk about their trips to the grocery store. With whom do they go? How often do they go? Do they get to help shop? What parts of the store do they like best? Pantomime and narrate an imaginary trip to the store to help children visualize the aisles, the products, and the activity inside of the store. Pick out juicy oranges, the biggest box of spaghetti, cold, cold milk, and plump, ripe tomatoes.

groceries, fresh produce—fruits and vegetables, canned goods, frozen foods, meat and poultry; counter, dairy foods, check-out, cashier, grocery cart, bag, sale, prices, clerk

- Use topically related books, such as those in the list that follows, in introducing the center and during its use. Book-related activities should include reading aloud to children and opportunities for them to explore the books on their own.
- Take a trip to a grocery store. Note signs on windows and signs inside the store.
- Provide play foods, empty food boxes and cans, and paper bags for purchases.
- Decide on a name for the store. If it is appropriate to your setting, create a store that specializes in ethnic foods, such as Indian, Chinese, or Polish. Make a sign with the name of the store and signs and posters giving information about specials or sales.
- Make labels for products, such as soup, fruit, cereal, dairy, noodles. Have children take turns classifying and ordering containers, grouping them according to the labels.
- Make price tags for items on sale.
- Have partners read the print and identify letters on cereal boxes. Then have them make up their own cereals, creating construction paper wrappers.
- Encourage children to contribute their favorite cereal boxes to the store. Write the names of the cereals on a graph and tally the choices in order to determine a class favorite.
- Read the ingredients listed on canned and boxed foods with children and have them decide which foods are the best for them to eat.
- Provide customers with play money for making their purchases. You may want to have check blanks available, too, reminding children that this is another way to pay for what you buy.
- Use Blackline Master 9, *Shopping List* and *Receipt*. Model how telephone orders are taken and recorded using a chalkboard version of the customer order form found on this Blackline Master. Again using a chalkboard model, show children how a salesperson might fill out a receipt. Then encourage children to use these forms in the center, with either real or pretend words and numbers.

tables	shelves or puppet stage for display	cardboard boxes
empty food containers	playdough or plastic foods	grocery bags
apron for storekeeper	broom	cash register
play money	telephone	
spray bottle of water and cloth for cleaning check-out counter		

pads of paper	store signs and posters	pencils
telephone book	advertisements	food labels
blank check forms	coupons from newspapers and magazines	
Blackline Master 9, *Shopping List, Receipt*		

BOOKS TO READ

Carrick, Donald. *Milk*. New York: Greenwillow, 1985. Beautiful illustrations and clear, direct text help children understand how milk is processed. (Preschool-1)

Caseley, Judith. *Grandpa's Garden Lunch*. New York: Greenwillow, 1990. After planting and caring for a garden, a child and her grandfather share a delicious vegetable garden lunch. (Preschool+)

Ehlert, Lois. *Growing Vegetable Soup*. San Diego: Harcourt, 1987. The author/illustrator's well-known graphics illustrate how vegetables are grown to go into delicious soup. (Preschool-3)

Friedman, Ina. *How My Parents Learned to Eat*. Ill. by Allen Say. New York: Houghton Mifflin, 1984. A warm story about eating customs told by a girl who has a Japanese mother and an American father. (Kindergarten-3)

Hutchins, Pat. *Don't Forget the Bacon!* New York: Greenwillow, 1976. Readers will relate to the boy who forgets his shopping list. A great play on words. (Kindergarten-3)

MacDonald, Elizabeth. *Mr. MacGregor's Breakfast Egg*. Ill. by Alex Ayliffe. New York: Viking, 1990. Everyone reads to find out if the hen will give the farmer his breakfast egg. (Preschool-1)

Pillar, Marjorie. *Pizza Man*. New York: Crowell, 1990. Black and white photographs show the step-by-step process of making a pizza. (Kindergarten-3)

Blackline Master 9

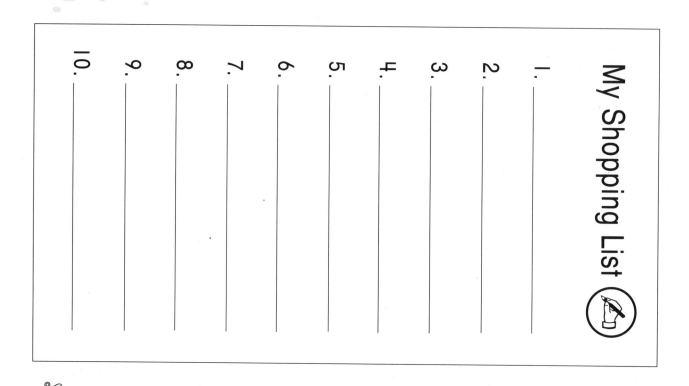

My Shopping List ✎

1. _____
2. _____
3. _____
4. _____
5. _____
6. _____
7. _____
8. _____
9. _____
10. _____

✂ -

Receipt

Item 1 _____ $_____

Item 2 _____ $_____

Item 3 _____ $_____

Item 4 _____ $_____

Item 5 _____ $_____

Total _____ $_____

Create a Pet Store

A classroom pet store may provide children with a unique, longed-for experience as they care for imaginary or stuffed-animal pets. Of course, nothing can compare to the experience of caring for and feeding a real, live classroom animal. Rabbits are nice.

Model Language

Engage children in a discussion about pet animals, encouraging those who have pets to talk about them—telling their names and describing them. If children have not had experience with pets, invite them to think about what kinds of animals would make good pets and to tell why they would like to have a specific animal as a pet. Read *Arthur's Pet Business* by Marc Brown (Little, Brown, 1990), *The Third-Story Cat* by Leslie Baker (Little, Brown, 1987), and Ruth Brown's *Our Puppy's Vacation* (Dutton, 1987). Visit a neighborhood pet store and then have children talk about the things they saw there: kinds of animals, animal foods, grooming supplies, toys, and pet accessories. Next, lead a brainstorming session on the things that could be placed in a classroom pet store. List categories on the chalkboard or make word webs.

Related Vocabulary & Concepts

animal, pet, grooming, coat, claws, purr, bark, caring for, leash, collar, tricks, kindness, friendship, pet supplies, and pet foods

- Use topically related books, such as those in the list that follows, in introducing the center and during its use. Book-related activities should include reading aloud to children and opportunities for them to explore the books on their own.
- Ask children to bring stuffed animals and pet accessories from home, such as leashes, a pet bed, toys, collars, pet dishes, combs, brushes, and empty pet food containers.
- Provide cardboard boxes or baskets to be used as pet cages. If it is not possible to set up a permanent pet store area, have children make pet cages using blocks. Display animal posters or pictures on the walls in the area.
- Encourage children to make a sign for the store as well as signs naming each of the animals, price tags, and pet shop posters.
- Provide a toy cash register and play money made by the children.
- Place pet training manuals and books about breeds of animals in the center. Several series about pets are available in libraries, such as the *First Pets* series by Kate Petty (Gloucester Press), covering gerbils, hamsters, kittens, puppies, ponies, and rabbits.
- Invite children to make their own pet food labels to cover empty food boxes and cans.
- Place Blackline Master 10, *Pet Store Receipt, Pet Supplies Checklist,* and *Healthy Pet Checklist.* Talk together about why taking care of a pet is a big responsibility—pets have to be given food and water every day, and many need daily exercise. Help children discover how a checklist like the one on the Blackline Master can be helpful as they care for their pets at home. Review the other forms, too, encouraging children to use them in the center with real or pretend writing.

Pet Store Equipment & Materials

stuffed animals	cardboard boxes	baskets
cash register	pet grooming supplies	leash
collar	empty pet food containers	pet toys
plastic food dishes	water bottles	blankets

Literacy Materials

play money	store signs	pads of paper and pencils
animal posters	price tags	sales receipts
check lists	pet owner manuals	pet breed pamphlets
labels for pet foods		

Blackline Master 10, *Pet Store Receipt, Healthy Pet Checklist, Pet Supplies Checklist*

Baker, Alan. *Benjamin's Portrait.* New York: Lothrop, Lee & Shepard, 1987. The antics of the lovable hamster in this book are especially interesting if a real hamster is available for observation and comparison. (Preschool-2)

Baker, Jeannie. *Home in the Sky.* New York: Greenwillow, 1984. The author's collage art illustrates a sensitive story about a boy and a pigeon. (Kindergarten-3)

Baker, Leslie. *The Third-Story Cat.* Boston: Little, Brown, 1987. Looking for adventure, an apartment cat wanders through the city but eventually returns to its comfortable home. (Preschool-3)

Bare, Colleen Stanley. *Guinea Pigs Don't Read Books.* New York: Putnam, 1985. The photographs in this book illustrate why guinea pigs are delightful pets. (Kindergarten-3)

Brown, Marc, *Arthur's Pet Business.* Boston: Little, Brown, 1990. Arthur has quite an adventure as he establishes a pet business. (Preschool-3)

Brown, Ruth. *Our Puppy's Vacation.* New York: Dutton, 1987. A warm portrayal of a puppy's first vacation in the English countryside. (Preschool-1)

Ehlert, Lois. *Feathers for Lunch.* San Diego: Harcourt, 1990. A beautifully designed book about a cat and neighborhood birds by an award-winning author/artist. (Preschool-3)

Griffith, Helen V. *Plunk's Dreams.* Ill. by Susan Condie Lamb. New York: Greenwillow, 1990. A boy imagines the exciting adventures his sleeping dog is dreaming about. (Preschool+)

Keats, Ezra Jack. *Whistle for Willie.* New York: Viking, 1964. This is not only a story about a boy and his dog, but about learning to whistle, too. (Preschool-1)

Khalsa, Dayal Kaur. *Julian.* New York: Crown, 1989. Until he learns good house manners, a large, lovable dog creates lots of trouble. (Gr. 1-3)

Blackline Master 1

Pet Store
135 Main Street
Downtown, U.S.A.

Quantity	Item	Price
	Tax	
	Total	

Customer _____

Our pets are perky and peppy!

✂ -

Healthy Pet Checklist

	time	date
fed pet		
changed water		
cleaned cage		
groomed pet		
exercised pet		

Pet Supplies Checklist

	have	need		have	need
bird cage			fish bowl		
bird seed			fish food		
brush			flea spray		
cat treats			hamster pellets		
cedar chips			kitty litter		
chew toy			leash		
collar			pet bed		
dog bones			pet dish		

Visit the Veterinarian's Office

Stuffed animals get sick, too. They need bandages and blankets, thermometers and medicine. Most of all, they need lots of love when they're feeling sick. Children practice nurturing and caring when they create a hospice for animals.

Model Language

Explain that an animal doctor is called a veterinarian and that when animals such as dog, cats, or birds are sick, people take them to the veterinarian's office. Because farm and many animals in zoos are often large and do not travel well, veterinarians usually go to the farm or zoo when these animals get sick. Have children name animals they think could be brought to an office and then name the animals that a veterinarian would have to visit in the zoo or on a farm. Write the word veterinarian on the chalkboard for children's reference. Brainstorm with children what happens when they go to the doctor's office, what they see in the waiting room and in the examining room. Help children make comparisons between their experiences and what happens when animals go to the veterinarian's office.

Related Vocabulary & Concepts

veterinarian, pets, farm animals, zoo animals, groomers, examining room, prescriptions, medicine, appointments, cages

- Use topically related books, such as those in the list that follows, in introducing the center and during its use. Book-related activities should include reading aloud to children and opportunities for them to explore the books on their own.

- Invite children to suggest equipment that should be included in a veterinarian's office and waiting room, such as an examining table, animal cages, doctor's supplies, and a doctor's kit for traveling to farms.

- Encourage children to make *environmental signs*, such as *The Doctor Is In, Office Hours, Cat Entrance, Dog Entrance*, and so on.

- Discuss with children the roles of the doctor, nurse, receptionist, and animal helpers.

- Model literacy activities, such as making appointments, checking patient folders and records, writing prescriptions, using the telephone, and describing patient symptoms to the doctor.

- Duplicate Blackline Master 11, *Appointment Card, Patient Record*, and *Prescription Pad*. Continue the comparisons between children's visits to a doctor and what happens in a veterinarian's office as you look together at the forms on the Blackline Master. Discuss why each form is used by doctors with patients—both animal and human—and show children how all three are filled out. Encourage children to practice their own writing (real or pretend) by using these forms in the center.

Veterinarian's Office Equipment & Materials

stuffed animals	cardboard box cages	table
waiting room chairs	telephone	animal dishes
grooming supplies	lab coats or smocks	flashlight
tongue depressors	thermometer	cotton balls
doctor's bag		

animal posters   pet pamphlets   magazines

telephone book   patient records and files   appointment book

prescription pad   paper, pencils   appointment cards

Blackline Master 11, *Appointment Card, Prescription Pad, Patient Record*

OOKS TO READ

Arnosky, Jim. *Raccoons and Ripe Corn.* New York: Lothrop, Lee & Shepard, 1987. Farms are home to many animals, even raccoons. This beautiful picture book tells of some raccoons' adventures at night. (Preschool-3)

Coxe, Molly. *Whose Footprints?* New York: Crowell, 1990. A mother and her daughter explore footprints in the snow as they guess which animals made them. (Preschool-1)

de Paola, Tomie. *Charlie Needs a Cloak.* New York: Simon & Schuster, 1982. This classic story shows the process involved in making clothing from a sheep's wool. (Kindergarten-4)

Ernst, Lisa Campbell. *When Bluebell Sang.* New York: Bradbury Press, 1989. When it is discovered that Bluebell the cow can sing, she and her owner go on a whirlwind tour of America. The homesick cow devises a plan that gets her back to the farm. (Preschool-2)

Heller, Ruth. *Chickens Aren't the Only Ones.* New York: Putnam, 1981. Readers may be surprised at how many animals, besides chickens, lay eggs. (Preschool-1)

Lauber, Patricia. *What's Hatching Out of That Egg?* New York: Crown, 1979. Readers will enjoy predicting what is coming out of the egg. (Gr. 2-4)

Petty, Kate. *First Pets Series.* New York: Gloucester Press, various dates. Interesting information about common pets is presented in an understandable way. (In the same series: *Gerbils, Hamsters, Kittens, Puppies,* and *Rabbits.*) (Gr. 1-3)

Royston, Angela. *Cow.* New York: Warwick Press, 1990. This series about farm animals includes photographs and has understandable text. (In the same series: *Goat, Hen, Pig, Pony,* and *Sheep.*) (Preschool-3)

Sproule, Michael and Sproule, Anna. *Cats.* New York: Watts, 1988. The text and photographs in this *Know Your Pet* series provide the reader with clear information about animals. (In the same series: *Dogs, Gerbils, Guinea Pigs, Hamsters, Mice and Rats,* and *Rabbits.*) (Gr. 1-6)

Blackline Master 1

Prescription

Has an appointment on

☐ Mon. ☐ Tues. ☐ Wed. ☐ Thurs. ☐ Fri. ☐ Sat.

Date _____ at _____ a.m.

p.m.

The Veterinarian's Office

Dr. Mary M. Verygood, D. V. M.

✂ -

Patient's name: _____

Prescription:

Refills:

Instructions:

The Veterinarian's Office

Dr. Mary M. Verygood, D. V. M.

Patient Record

Patient's name: _____ Type of animal: _____

Owner's Name: _____

Address: _____ Telephone number: _____

Date of visit	Observations	Treatment

Create a Zoo Store

After a field trip to the zoo, children will be eager to re-create what they experienced at the world's most exciting place. If a trip isn't possible, build background by providing lots of pictures and lots of conversation to stimulate imaginations.

Model Language

Invite children to talk about experiences they have had at a zoo. Encourage them to tell about their favorite animals, where they are housed and what the zoo looked like. Ask them to describe their experiences there, such as eating at a snack shop or watching animals being fed. If children have not had zoo experiences, display pictures, read books about zoos, and lead them on an imaginary trip to help them visualize the environment.

Related Vocabulary & Concepts

zoo, zoo keeper, animal trainer, wild animals, reptiles, large cats, birds, mammals, apes, marine animals, dolphin show, feeding, snack shop

- Use topically related books, such as those in the list that follows, in introducing the center and during its use. Book-related activities should include reading aloud to children and opportunities for them to explore the books on their own.

- Explain that most zoos have a store where people can buy stuffed animals, animal statues, jewelry, post cards, maps, books about animals, animal games, and puzzles.

- Establish the Zoo Store in the dramatic play area or out-of-doors. If there is space out-of-doors, have children make directional signs telling visitors where various animals are located in the zoo.

- Have children suggest items in the classroom that could be displayed in a zoo store, such as plastic or wooden zoo animals, animal books, magazines, animal lotto games, or animal picture cards.

- Have children suggest things that they can make to include in the store, such as posters, zoo pennants, pamphlets about animals, and signs for the store.

- Invite children to suggest names for a classroom store, such as *Fur and Feathers, The Crocodile Stop,* or *Elephant Crossing* and then vote on the name.

- Provide picture books of animals for children's reference.

- Have children make price tags for items to be sold.

- Provide paper and pencils so that children can make zoo maps.

- Model for children the questions customers might ask of a salesperson about materials available and the answers they might receive.

- Model the use of literacy materials in the center, such as reading animal pamphlets, and zoo signs and using zoo maps.

- Use Blackline Master 12, *Zoo Store Sales Receipt* and *Animal Facts Sheet.* Begin by talking about why customers want receipts when they buy things and why salespeople agree that they are important. Show children how a receipt would be filled out for several purchases in a center store. Ask them to use the receipts, too, as they play in the center. Assure them that they can use either real or pretend words and numbers. In modeling the use of the Animal Facts Sheet, base your responses on your own pet, if possible, or the pet of one of the children.

tables	shelves or display counters	cash register
telephone	stuffed animals	plastic or wooden animals
animal lotto games	animal puzzles	

animal magazines	animal books	zoo posters
zoo pennants	store signs	sales receipts
paper, pencils	maps, zoo guides	animal stamps/pads

Blackline Master 12, *Zoo Store Sales Receipt, Animal Facts Sheet*

BOOKS TO READ

Anno, Mitsumasa. *Anno's Masks*. New York: Philomel, 1990. A good book to read before making animal masks. The clear illustrations capture the essence of each animal. (Preschool-K)

Barrett, Norman. *Picture Library—Elephants*. New York: Watts, 1990. Take a close look at elephants in this book. (Others in the series include: *Picture Library: Big Cats, Picture Library: Monkeys & Apes, Picture Library: Pandas,* and *Picture Library: Polar Animals*.) (Kindergarten-3)

Demi. *Demi's Count the Animals 1-2-3*. New York: Grosset & Dunlap, 1986. The poetic text and detailed illustrations make this an animal book to linger over. (Preschool-2)

Ehlert, Lois. *Color Zoo*. New York: Lippincott, 1989. This 1990 Caldecott Honor Book shows the unique features of zoo animals. (Preschool-1)

Guarino, Deborah. *Is Your Mama a Llama?* Ill. by Steven Kellogg. New York: Scholastic, 1989. Children will chime in the reading as they predict text and enjoy the rhyme and repetition in this delightful story. (Preschool-2)

Hadithi, Mwenye. *Greedy Zebra*. Ill. by Adrienne Kennaway. Boston: Little, Brown, 1984. An African tale that explains why the zebra has such a distinctive coat. (Preschool-3)

Hoban, Tana. *A Children's Zoo*. New York: Greenwillow, 1985. Stunning black and white photographs of animals entice the viewer to visit a zoo. (Preschool-1)

Jonas, Ann. *The Trek*. New York: Greenwillow, 1985. A daily walk to school becomes a safari adventure as a girl imagines wild animals in her neighborhood. (Kindergarten-3)

Jorgensen, Gail. *Crocodile Beat*. Ill. by Patricia Mullins. New York: Bradbury Press, 1989. Jungle animals dance and play, chatter and roar. Children will enjoy the crocodile's surprise at the end of this rhyming book. (Preschool-1)

Blackline Master 12

The Zoo Store
Exotic Animal Gifts
from Around the World

Quantity	Item	Price
	Tax	
	Total	

Received by:

- - ✂ -

Animal Facts Sheet

Animal's name:

Where animal is found:

land [ ]   sea [ ]   air [ ]

Size of animal:

little [ ]   big [ ]   very big [ ]

Color: gray [ ]   white [ ]   brown [ ]   black [ ]   red [ ]   yellow [ ]

Description:

What animal eats:

Visit a Travel Agency

Everybody loves to talk about their adventures and travels. When setting up a travel agency environment, invite parents to contribute posters, souvenirs, and photographs from trips they have taken. Invite guest speakers to share their experiences.

Before setting up a travel agency dramatic play center, children will need to understand the purposes and functions of travel agencies. Invite children to share experiences they have had preparing for and going on trips with family members or friends. List on the chalkboard places children have gone and record the method of transportation used—car, train, plane, or boat. Talk about the services that travel agencies provide, such as arranging for tours, transportation, and hotel accommodations. Encourage children to talk about experiences they have had staying at hotels or motels. Brainstorm with children about the places to which they would like to travel. Tell children about trips you have taken and show them pictures of your travels.

travel, travel agent, customer, trip, transportation, reservations, hotel, airplane, car, train, boat, map, country, city, tour

- Use topically related books, such as those in the list that follows, in introducing the center and during its use. Book-related activities should include reading aloud to children and opportunities for them to explore the books on their own.

- Provide a table and chairs, a typewriter, a telephone, a real or pretend computer, and writing materials.

- Provide travel brochures, available at local travel agencies, and magazines featuring travel so that children will have a broader idea of places to travel.

- Introduce reference books that show pictures of tourist attractions in the United States and books such as the *We Live In* series published by Franklin Watts and the *I N S I D E Countries* series, also published by Watts.

- Provide various types of maps for children to read and display. If a world map is available, designate where children live and help them locate where they plan to travel.

- Collect travel sections from newspapers and encourage children to make travel scrapbooks.

- Encourage children to share photographs of trips they have taken.

- Invite children to make travel posters to display in the agency.

- Model for children the conversation that a travel agent might have with clients, determining where the clients want to travel, the dates of the trip, method of transportation, tour, hotel, and meal arrangements.

- Provide Blackline Master 13, *My Travel Agency,* so that agents can make arrangements in the center. Show children how the form on Blackline Master 13 can be used to record the plans.

- After children have had opportunities to look at travel brochures and picture books featuring countries around the world, have the class vote on a place to take an imaginary trip. Find out interesting information about the place and then plan for the trip by making plane tickets, arranging chairs to resemble the inside of a plane, designating flight attendants and captain, and so on. Pantomime the plane flight and lead children on an imaginary tour when they reach their destination, helping them visualize the location.

Travel Agency
Center
Equipment
& Materials

Literacy
Materials

table	chairs	typewriter
telephone	toy airplanes, cars, ships, trains	computer
chairs for clients	cardboard boxes for brochures and magazines	

travel posters	travel brochures	trip photographs
maps	telephone book	pads of paper
pencils	child-made plane tickets	travel sections from newspapers
Blackline Master 13, *My Travel Agency*		

BOOKS TO READ

Barracca, Debra, and Barracca, Sal. *The Adventures of Taxi Dog*. Ill. by Mark Buchner. New York: Dial, 1990. A taxi driver and his lovable dog lead the reader through a rollicking adventure on wheels. (Preschool-3)

Crews, Donald. *Truck*. New York: Greenwillow, 1980. This almost wordless book is filled with environmental print on trucks, billboards, and road signs. (Preschool-2)

Kovalski, Maryann. *The Wheels on the Bus*. Boston: Little, Brown, 1987. The traditional song is told with a delightful new twist as a grandma and her granddaughters, who are having such fun singing, miss the bus. (Preschool-4)

McPhail, David. *Ed and Me*. San Diego: Harcourt, 1990. A father shares stories with his daughter about a beloved farm pick-up truck. (Preschool-3)

Maestro, Betsy. *Taxi: A Book of City Words*. Ill. by Giulio Maestro. New York: Clarion, 1989. Words about the city are introduced as the reader follows a busy taxi through the day. (Preschool-2)

Magee, Doug. *All Aboard ABC*. New York: Dutton, 1990. Children will learn all about trains as they look at this collection of train terms and photographs. (Preschool-1)

Rockwell, Anne. *Cars*. New York: Dutton, 1984. The text in this book is simple but informative. (Preschool-1)

Wolcott, Patty. *Double-Decker, Double-Decker, Double-Decker Bus*. Ill. by Bob Barner. New York: Random House, 1991. A perfect book for beginning readers. (Preschool-2)

Blackline Master 13

My Travel Agency

Travel Plan Form

Name(s): _____

Want to go to: _____

By: plane   car   train   bus

When: _____

Will stay at: hotel   motel   bed and breakfast

Will eat: breakfast   lunch   dinner

Travel Plan completed by _____

Work at the Office

Children are intrigued by the work that adults do. They are impressed with the importance of going to a job every day. Materials that are commonplace for adults are fascinating for children. Watch them delight in paper clips, staplers, steno pads, and thin, yellow pencils with erasers.

Invite children to discuss the jobs adults in their families do. Lead children to understand that many people work in offices and do different kinds of work. Encourage children who have family members who work in offices to find out more about what kinds of things they do when they are at work. Invite a parent to come to class to talk about his or her job in an office and describe the work and the equipment. If possible, visit a large office complex. Model how to make a telephone call; how to take messages and/or orders on a telephone; how to use the telephone book to look up numbers; how to schedule meetings.

Related
Vocabulary
& Concepts

work, jobs, office, building, telephone, typewriter, computer, files, desk, copy machine, elevator, business

- Use topically related books, such as those in the list that follows, in introducing the center and during its use. Book-related activities should include reading aloud to children and opportunities for them to explore the books on their own.

- Visit the school office and the principal's office. Have the staff show children the machines used there, such as computers, typewriters, telephones, answering machines, the intercom system, copiers, and calculators.

- Provide empty cardboard boxes, cartons, and tubes so that children can make machines for their office. After machines are assembled, have children paint them, designating keyboards, dials, and switches.

- If possible, provide used typewriters, adding machines, or telephones. Demonstrate how to make telephones using juice cans and string.

- Encourage family members to donate surplus office forms, used computer paper, junk mail, and envelopes.

- Have children make signs for the office including company names, name labels for desks, *No Smoking* signs, and signs designating the *Copy Room, Switchboard,* and *Receptionist.*

- Provide pads and sheets of paper, writing tools, rubber stamps, paper clips, rubber bands, tape, staplers, and scissors.

- Encourage children to put written materials into notebooks or binders and demonstrate how alphabet letters are written on cards or sheets of paper to make file boxes. Provide shoe boxes to be used for filing materials.

- Use Blackline Master 14, *Telephone Message* and *Appointment Schedule.* Show children how each form is used after discussing the importance to adult workers of relaying messages and keeping schedules straight. Encourage children to include these forms in their play, using either real or pretend words and numbers.

Office
Equipment
& Materials

chairs	table	used office machines
typewriter	computer	file boxes
notebooks	child-made machines	telephone or play phones
stapler	paper clips	rubber bands

pads, sheets of paper   pens, pencils   notebook paper

child-made charts   child-made office signs   surplus office forms

computer paper   graph paper   telephone book

boxes for filing   alphabet filing cards

Blackline Master 14, *Telephone Message, Appointment Schedule*

BOOKS TO READ

Allen, Jeffrey. *Mary Alice, Operator Number 9.* Ill. by James Marshall. Boston: Little, Brown, 1975. Mary Alice is a very funny telephone operator who could only have been created by James Marshall. (Gr. 1-3)

Barton, Byron. *Machines at Work.* New York: Crowell, 1987. Machines, jobs people do, and colors are all concepts that can be taught when reading this book. (Preschool-1)

Cobb, Vicki. *Skyscraper Going Up!* Ill. by John Strajan. New York: Crowell, 1987. A three-dimensional book that clearly shows the construction process of a high-rise building. (Gr. 1-5)

Rockwell, Anne. *Come to Town.* New York: Crowell, 1987. The school, grocery store, an office, and a library are featured in this community of bears. (Preschool-Kindergarten)

Rockwell, Anne and Rockwell, Harlow. *Machines.* New York: Macmillan, 1972. Clear illustrations and brief text show machines and how they work. (Preschool-1)

Steig, William. *Doctor DeSoto.* New York: Farrar, Straus & Giroux, 1982. The mouse dentist is up to his famous tricks when his fox patient comes to his office with a toothache. (Kindergarten-2)

Stickland, Paul. *Machines as Big as Monsters.* New York: Random House, 1989. Detailed illustrations show the overwhelming size and strength of earth-moving machines. (Kindergarten-3)

Williams, Vera B. *A Chair for My Mother.* New York: Greenwillow, 1982. A little girl and her mother work hard to save money for a special chair. Readers can compare working in an office with working in a restaurant as the characters in this book do. (Kindergarten-3)

Blackline Master 14

☎

To _____

Date _____

Time _____

While You Were Out

Name _____

Phone Number _____

Please Phone ☐

Will Call Again ☐

See Me ☐

Message _____

_____

_____

Message Taken By

Appointments

Monday	🕐
Tuesday	🕐
Wednesday	🕐
Thursday	🕐
Friday	🕐
Saturday	🕐
Sunday	🕐

From *Just Pretend!* by Judy Nyberg. Copyright © 1994 GoodYearBooks.

Design an Astronaut Center

Young children's understanding of the moon, stars, space, and space travel has been affected by the advent of America's space program. Let their imaginations soar in an astronaut center or a skylab.

Children will begin to understand the concepts of astronauts and space travel when they look at the photographs and illustrations in books, such as the *New True Book* series, published by Childrens Press, with titles including *Spacelab, Skylab,* and *Moon Flights.* As children look at these and other topically related books, talk about astronauts' special clothing and equipment. Describe how space shuttles look inside and outside. Show children photographs featuring space shuttle flight decks and command center control rooms and then talk about their complexity. Brainstorm with children what an astronaut center should include. Let children decide if their center should feature a command center with monitors and tracking panels, a training area for astronauts to practice weightlessness and exercise, or a spacecraft flight deck. Let children decide on a classroom location for the center and share in making plans for its size.

astronaut, space, earth, space craft, spacesuit, command center, weightlessness, control panel, power, on/off, flag, planets, moon, rocket, fuel, satellite

- Books and illustrations from other sources will be especially important in helping children enjoy this center to the fullest. See the list on page 59 for specific suggestions.
- Remind children that the Kennedy Space Center is named after a United States President; then have children decide on a name for their center.
- Provide cardboard boxes which children can use in making monitors, panels, or flight decks. Use aluminum foil and construction paper for dials and meters.
- After looking at photographs of spacesuits, have children make astronaut clothing using large paper bags or white shirts or pillowcases.
- Space helmets can be made by spray painting grocery bags with silver paint. Cut out a frame for the face and cover with cellophane.
- Provide gloves and boots for astronaut suits. Underwater face masks and bicycle helmets can be worn if available.
- Turn children's backpacks into Portable Life Support Systems (PLSS).
- Have children use walkie-talkies as a communication system, or make a system using small boxes.
- Have astronauts practice dexterity by moving objects from one container to another with kitchen tongs.
- Simulate weightlessness training on pillowed areas.
- Have children make signs for control panels, such as *on-off, power switch, blast-off, ignition,* or *Training Center.*
- Encourage children to make pennants or flags to be raised when astronauts land on a planet.

- Use Blackline Master 15, *My Flight Plan* and *My Daily Log,* to record activities. Describe for children why astronauts carefully record what they do during space flights. Their information is used to help all of us learn more about space. The flight plan is necessary, too, not only to the astronauts, but to the people on earth who are looking out for their safety. Show children how each form might be completed, and urge them to use the forms, too, as they play in the center. The words and numbers they use can be either real or pretend. It's the concept of writing information that's important.

chairs	work tables	cardboard boxes
aluminum foil	construction paper	shirts for spacesuits
bicycle helmets	face masks	boots
gloves	pillows, cushions	
shelves or bookcases for control panels		

picture books	paper and writing tools	astronaut center signs
construction paper for flags and planets		notebooks for logs and journaling
Blackline Master 15, *My Flight Plan, My Daily Log*		

BOOKS TO READ

- Barton, Byron. *I Want to Be an Astronaut.* New York: Crowell, 1988. The author/illustrator's bold designs illustrate the activities of a would-be astronaut. (Preschool-1)

- Fradin, Dennis. *A New True Book—Moon Flights.* Chicago: Childrens Press, 1985. The easy-to-understand text and accompanying photographs help young readers visualize concepts about space travel. See other *New True Books: Spacelab* and *Skylab.* (Gr. 1-4)

- Furniss, Tim. *The First Men on the Moon.* Ill. by Peter Bull. New York: Watts, 1989. This book follows the training and experiences of the astronauts on the Apollo 11 mission to the moon. The photographs in this book will enhance children's understanding of the concepts of astronauts and space travel. (Gr. 4-6)

- Graham, Ian. *How It Works—Space Shuttles.* Ill. by Ron Hayward. New York: Gloucester Press, 1989. Readers will enjoy the detailed diagrams of space shuttles. (Gr. 5-6)

- McPhail, David. *First Flight.* Boston: Little, Brown, 1987. On his first plane trip, a boy observes safety rules and good manners although his teddy bear companion forgets. (Preschool-3)

Blackline Master 15

My Flight Plan

Astronaut's Name

Date of Flight

Destination

My Daily Log

Astronaut

Date

Today I

Date

Today I

Date

Today I

Play at a Sandy Beach

Here comes the sand and the water! Sand and water play fix up bad days and provide endless hours of contentment and satisfaction. Grab your beach ball and towel. Don't forget the picnic! Let's go to the beach!

Read books about the beach, such as *Beach Ball* by Peter Sis (Greenwillow, 1990), *A Beach Day* by Douglas Florian (Greenwillow, 1990), *One Sun—A Book of Terse Verse* by Bruce McMillan (Holiday House, 1990), or *Morning Beach* by Leslie Baker (Little, Brown, 1990). Help children visualize the experience of being at a beach by taking an imaginary trip. Pack your picnic lunch, your towel, and bathing suit. Don't forget the sunscreen cream! Look at the sparkling water, the beach umbrellas, and all the colors of the towels and bathing suits. Feel the sun on your back and the hot sand on your feet. Now, let's run down to the water! Have children join in the dialogue and tell how and what they are feeling. Encourage children to talk about experiences they have had at the beach. Invite them to plan a day at the beach, telling what they would do to get ready for the trip and what they would do once they get there.

water, sand, beach, bathing suit, beach towel, swimming, running, playing, safety, picnic, beach umbrella, rocks, shells, boats, seagulls, sandpipers, pelicans

Young children enjoy playing with sand and water. The physical properties of the materials provide varied opportunities for experimentation and exploration as children fill containers, mix, measure, and delight in the textures. Children who do not have access to beaches or bodies of water will especially enjoy experiencing these materials. Sheets of plastic or drop cloths placed underwater and sand tables assure speedy clean-up and confine materials to a specific area. If sand and water tables are not available, dish pans work well. Some teachers successfully use small plastic wading pools as indoor sand boxes. Sand and water activities are also appropriate for out-of-doors play. When using sand and water, children need clear guidelines regarding expectations and behaviors.

- Let children suggest a name for a beach to be established near the sand and water tables. Have children make signs for dressing rooms, refreshment stands, and parking.
- Provide a stool for a lifeguard station and label with a sign.
- Create a hot dog or an ice-cream stand, making appropriate signs and posters.
- Display a list of beach safety rules, such as Do Not Swim Alone and NO DOGS ALLOWED.
- Have a shell treasure hunt by placing shells or stones in the sand and letting children take turns digging them up, recording how many they find.
- Model for children how people spend time at the beach reading books and magazines, writing letters, and playing board or card games.
- Provide Blackline Master 16, *Things I Need for the Beach* and *A Day at the Beach* recording experiences. Work together to complete a model of each on the chalkboard. Then urge children to use these forms during their play, practicing writing with real or invented spelling.
- Invite children to suggest items needed for a beach party. List on the board suggestions, such as beach towels, bathing suits, beach balls, pails and shovels, and picnic food in a basket. (You may want to incorporate the form *Things I Need for the Beach* here.)

- Designate a day as "Beach Party Day." Have children help compose a letter informing parents about the day as you write the information on a chart.
- Celebrate the event by wearing bathing suits. Spread out beach towels, have a fruit snack, and play music on a radio.
- Compare colors in beach towels and play a color-search game using the towels.
- Play relay races or circle games with beach balls.
- Throughout the use of this center, continue to provide related books for children to read and explore.

sand table	water table	plastic wading pool
dish pans	plastic sheets or drop cloths	aprons for water play
sponges	shells, rocks	water toys
pails and shovels	beach towels	beach balls
squeeze bottles for sunscreen cream		an umbrella to shade babies

books and magazines	travel posters	child-made signs
chart of beach rules	games for playing at the beach	

paper and pencils to record activities and write letters

Blackline Master 16, *Things I Need for the Beach, My Day at the Beach*

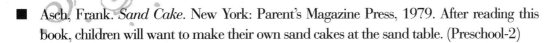

BOOKS TO READ

- Asch, Frank. *Sand Cake.* New York: Parent's Magazine Press, 1979. After reading this book, children will want to make their own sand cakes at the sand table. (Preschool-2)

- Baker, Leslie. *Morning Beach.* Boston: Little, Brown, 1990. Lovely water color paintings accompany a story about a girl and her mother sharing their first day at the beach in Maine. (Preschool-3)

- Florian, Douglas. *Beach Day.* New York: Greenwillow, 1990. A brief rhyming text and colorful illustrations make this a perfect book to introduce concepts about the beach. (Preschool+)

- Hartman, Gail. *For Sandcastles or Seashells.* Ill. by Ellen Weiss. New York: Bradbury Press, 1990. Simple captions define activities that children experience at the beach. (Preschool) Fairclough. New York: Franklin Watts, 1987. This book illustrates floating and sinking experimentation at the water table. (Kindergarten-3)

- Rylant, Cynthia. *Henry and Mudge and the Forever Sea: The Sixth Book of Their Adventures.* Ill. by Sucie Stevenson. New York: Bradbury, 1989. The boy and his dog experience together the joys of being at the beach. (Gr. 1-3)

Blackline Master 16

Things I need for the beach.

1.

2.

3.

4.

5.

- - ✂ -

Dear Diary,

My Day at the Beach

by _____

Go on a Deep-Sea Dive

Divers always sign in before a dive. Divers always dive with a partner. Divers always check out their equipment. Divers take turns looking for sunken treasure. Now, get ready for a great underwater adventure. "Wow! Look at that fish!

Before creating an undersea environment, make available resource books on undersea life and subterranean vehicles, such as *A New True Book—Dangerous Fish* (Childrens Press, 1982) and *Discovering Jellyfish* (Watts, 1989). Draw children's attention to how illustrators such as Lois Ehlert (*Fish Eyes: A Book You Can Count On,* Harcourt, 1990) and Eric Maddern (*Curious Clownfish,* Little, Brown, 1990) draw fish and undersea life. When looking at picture books with children, encourage them to talk about what they see in the illustrations and to ask questions. Help children make comparisons and relate new information to what they already know. Have you ever seen a fish that has so many colors? What kinds of fish have you seen? A goldfish? A fish you caught? A fish in the grocery store? Children who have not experienced water environments or marine animals will need many exposures to picture books and to descriptive oral language. (Additional title suggestions follow.) Take children on an imaginary deep-sea dive and describe what you see under the water or go on an imaginary submarine ride.

dive, diver, diving equipment, submarine, sea, ocean, seaweed, coral, rocks, schools of fish, shark, whale

- Invite children to brainstorm where in the classroom an underwater environment could be set up—in the block area, under an adult-sized table, or in a corner of the room where a sheet becomes a ceiling for the area.

- Provide large sheets of paper on which children can paint background water and under-sea plants.

- Encourage children to look at pictures of fish and other marine life before using construction paper collage or paints to create their own. When fish are completed, attach them to the ceiling of the environment as well as on background walls. Have children label the species of fish they have made.

- Provide underwater equipment, such as a face mask, snorkel tube, swim fins, and a flash-light.

- Encourage children to make oxygen tanks using cardboard tubes secured together with elastic bands or shoelaces.

- Provide paper and writing materials so that children can make a sign-in station for deep sea divers and underwater maps. Of course, divers use a buddy system.

- Provide a stopwatch or timer so that an above-water observer can record diving time to ensure a safe supply of oxygen.

- If children are interested, pursue the possibility of creating a submarine vehicle from card-board cartons.

- Use Blackline Master 17, *Diver's Equipment Checklist* and *Diver's Log,* for recording species of marine life. Help children understand why real divers might want and need to use a checklist and a log. Encourage children to practice their own writing as they play in the center, using real or pretend words and numbers.

table for displaying underwater equipment		chairs for above-water observers
face mask	swim fins	snorkel tube
flashlight	timer	cardboard tubes for oxygen tanks
elastic bands	shoelaces	sheet
large paper for background		

reference books	picture books	paper
underwater maps	drawing, painting materials	scissors
pads of paper for journaling		
Blackline Master 17, *Diver's Equipment Checklist, Diver's Log*		

BOOKS TO READ

Burningham, John. *Mr. Gumpy's Outing.* New York: Holt, 1971. The guests—all land creatures—aboard Mr. Gumpy's boat have a unique outing. (Preschool-1)

Ehlert, Lois. *Fish Eyes: A Book You Can Count On.* San Diego: Harcourt, 1990. In this colorful book, spotted, striped, smiling, fantailed fish are waiting to be counted. (Preschool-1)

Kalan, Robert. *Blue Sea.* Ill. by Donald Crews. New York: Greenwillow, 1979. Big and little fish swim across the pages of this book and invite readers to come along on an undersea adventure. (Kindergarten-3)

Koch, Michelle. *By the Sea.* New York: Greenwillow, 1991. This book shows the concept of opposites at the seashore using one word of text per page. (Preschool)

Lionni, Leo. *Fish Is Fish.* New York: Pantheon, 1970. A fish, jealous of a frog who jumps out of the pond, learns that he must live in the water. (Kindergarten-3)

_____. *Swimmy* (reissued ed.). New York: Knopf, 1973. Swimmy learns how to fool the big fish so that his school of red fish can explore the waters. (Preschool-1)

MacCarthy, Patricia. *Ocean Parade.* New York: Dial, 1990. The concepts of colors, size, and shape are reinforced with this aquatic adventure. (Preschool-1)

Maddern, Eric. *Curious Clownfish.* Ill. by Adrienne Kennaway. Boston: Little, Brown, 1990. Bright illustrations accompany this story about an adventurous clownfish who happily returns to its sea anemone home. (Preschool-3)

Blackline Master 17

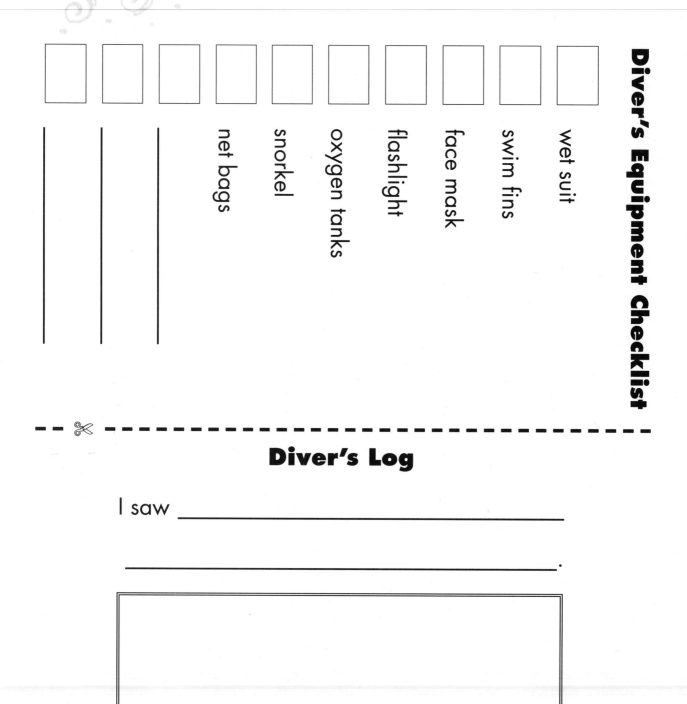

Diver's Equipment Checklist

wet suit

swim fins

face mask

flashlight

oxygen tanks

snorkel

net bags

✂ -

Diver's Log

I saw _____

_____.

Make A Classroom Aquarium

"The sharks are fed at 10:00 a.m. and 2:00 p.m. The penguins go on parade this afternoon. Over in this tank, ladies and gentlemen, are dangerous jellyfish and terrible stingrays. Keep your fingers out of the water. Don't forget to look at the seals play on your way out." What a cool place!

Children will benefit by visiting an aquarium where they can see a unique environment that will stimulate their own dramatic play. A trip to a pet store where tropical fish are featured can also be beneficial. Before going on a trip, encourage children to predict what they think they will see. After returning from a trip, give children many opportunities to recall their experiences and to tell about what they saw. Read *My Camera: At the Aquarium* by Janet Perry Marshall (Little, Brown, 1989) and then involve the whole class in a discussion about the kinds of animals they would see at an aquarium. Write children's suggestions on the board. As children think about creating an environment for marine animals, explain that some aquariums concentrate on displaying small fish and mammals while others—oceanariums—have large spaces for whales, sharks, seals, and penguins. Let children decide what kind of space is possible for use in their classroom.

aquarium, oceanarium, museum, tanks, marine biologist, entrance, exit, octopus, eel, fish, mammals, penguin, turtle, oxygen, feeding

- Provide picture and reference books about pond and sea animals so that children can use the illustrations as models when they make their own animals and fish from paper, clay, or collage materials. Several suggested titles follow.
- Encourage children to label the pictures and models of the animals they have created and to write fact sheets about each species.
- Demonstrate how cardboard boxes and meat trays covered with plastic wrap can be used to resemble fish tanks. When completed, stack boxes to display and attach meat-tray fish tanks to bulletin boards.
- Encourage children to make posters featuring animals and signs about dolphin shows, turtle eggs hatching, or polliwog-frog displays.
- Use resource materials to determine the measurements of large and small marine animals, such as whales, dolphins, tuna fish, turtles, frogs, and minnows, and then have children make masking-tape lines on a wall display to show the sizes of the animals.
- Have children make clay turtles and eggs, and have museum visitors estimate or count the number of eggs each turtle is hatching.
- Make directional signs such as *Entrance, Exit, Move This Way,* and signs that give information about feeding times.
- Invite children to make maps of the aquarium for visitors to use.
- Have children make tickets for entrance to the aquarium and brochures to be passed out to visitors.
- Provide a hat and a smock for aquarium guards and smocks for museum guides.
- Encourage children to take turns guiding visitors through the exhibits, giving information about the animals.

- Use Blackline Master 18, *Name the Baby* and *Animal Care* Record. Explain that often in a zoo or an aquarium, the workers and visitors are asked to help name a new baby animal when it is born. Look together at the Name the Baby form and make sure children know what each of the animals and fish is. Ask children to think of names that would be best for each. Provide time for sharing the suggestions. Also, discuss why workers in an aquarium would need a care record as they work. Explain that each animal is different, with its own food, its own schedule, and so on. Encourage children to use this form as they play in the center and care for their animals.

Aquarium Equipment & Materials

tables, shelves, or blocks for display tanks		cardboard boxes
meat/produce trays	plastic wrap	tape
smocks	hats	masking tape

Literacy Materials

posters	child-made signs	tickets
brochures	fact sheets	aquarium maps

Blackline Master 18, *Name the Baby; Animal Care Record*

BOOKS TO READ

- Koch, Michelle. *By the Sea.* New York: Greenwillow, 1991. This book shows the concept of opposites at the seashore using one word of text per page. (Preschool+)

- Lacey, Elizabeth A. *The Complete Frog; A Guide for the Very Young Naturalist.* Ill. by Christopher Santoro. New York: Lothrop, Lee & Shepard, 1989. Detailed drawings define the differences between toads and frogs. (Kindergarten-4)

- Marshall, Janet Perry. *My Camera: At the Aquarium.* Boston: Little, Brown, 1989. On each page, the reader guesses what the camera is viewing at the aquarium and then guesses are confirmed. (Preschool -2)

- Parker, Nancy Winslow. *Frogs, Toads, Lizards, and Salamanders.* Ill. by Joan Richards Wright. New York: Greenwillow, 1990. Here is an informative book that is enjoyable to read. (Gr. 1-4)

- Raffi. *Baby Beluga.* Ill. by Ashley Wolff. New York: Crown, 1990 (text © 1980, 1988 Troubadour Records; illustrations © 1990). The song's rhyming text offers an inviting opportunity for a shared reading experience. (Preschool-2)

Blackline Master 18

Name the Baby

✂ -

Animal Care Record

Kind of Animal	Tank Cleaned	Fed	How Much?
_____	☐	☐	_____
_____	☐	☐	_____
_____	☐	☐	_____

Set Up A Weather Station

"If it rains, we stay indoors. If it's cold, you have to wear your coats. If it's sunny, we can go on our picnic." No wonder children are interested in the weather. It affects their lives every day. Encourage them to become weather watchers, cartographers, and broadcasters.

Observing the weather and seasonal changes often becomes a part of the daily classroom routine when working with young children. Give children opportunities to talk about the weather by describing what they see and how it feels outside. Invite children to predict what they think the weather will be like the next day. Encourage them to watch a weather report on television or listen to a weather report on a radio so that they begin to understand the concept of predicting or forecasting weather. On the following day, have children compare the prediction they heard with actual weather conditions. If children watched a TV report, have them describe what they saw, such as a map of the country, temperatures listed, weather words, satellite pictures of clouds. Talk about the reasons people might want to predict the weather: planning for a picnic or trip, dressing appropriately for the day, and so on. Invite children to suggest what they would include in a classroom weather station, such as thermometers, charts, graphs for recording weather, and maps.

Related
Vocabulary
& Concepts

weather, map, report, prediction, forecast, weather station, clouds, sun, rain, storm, snow, hot/cold, wind, pollution, thermometer

- Use topically related books, such as those in the list that follows, in introducing the center and during its use. Book-related activities should include reading aloud to children and opportunities for them to explore the books on their own.
- Set up the weather station near a window for outdoor observation.
- Suggest some experiments for children to conduct, such as melting ice cubes on a sunshine-filled windowsill and in a darker location; collecting rainfall in plastic containers and measuring amounts; placing thermometers in cups of warm and cold water and then comparing the temperatures.
- Display commercial maps on walls and invite children to make their own maps.
- Invite children to look at cloud formations and record sightings on cloud-watch charts.
- Have children make weekly sun/cloud/rain/wind charts to record daily weather changes.
- Encourage children to make signs for the weather station, such as *Weather Alert, Weather Bulletin, Weather Forecast, Pollution* or *Ozone Alert.*
- Provide a large weather forecast chart where all forecasters can record their prediction for the next day's weather.
- Provide rulers, protractors, compasses, and other adultlike writing tools for children to chart and graph on large sheets of paper.
- Invite forecasters to interview classmates to determine how many were prepared for the day's weather and dressed accordingly.
- Provide copies of Blackline Master 19, *Today's Weather.* Begin by filling one form in together. Help children find where their city would be on the map. Together, choose three other cities to record. Once children understand how the map is used, encourage them to use additional maps over the next few days, recording actual temperatures and conditions (or, if more appropriate, what children imagine them to be).

table	chairs	classroom window
containers for water	maps	indoor and outdoor thermometers
barometer	weather page from local newspapers	

weather maps	protractors, compasses, rulers	weather signs
charts	pencils and other writing tools	
Blackline Master 19, *Today's Weather*		

BOOKS TO READ

Borden, Louise. *Caps, Hats, Socks, and Mittens.* Ill. by Lillian Hoban. New York: Scholastic, 1989. This delightful book, written in rhyme, highlights the changing seasons. (Preschool-2)

Florian, Douglas. *A Summer Day.* New York: Greenwillow, 1988. The author's brief, rhyming text and crayon illustrations capture the essence of the season and invite shared reading. See also *A Winter Day.* (Preschool-1)

Hirschi, Ron. *Spring.* Photographs by Thomas D. Mangelson. New York: Dutton, 1990. This collection of beautiful photographs shows animals in their mountain environment at the beginning of spring. (Preschool-3)

Keats, Ezra Jack. *The Snowy Day.* New York: Viking, 1962. The classic Caldecott Medal winner continues to delight readers with its simplicity and design. (Preschool-1)

Maass, Robert. *When Autumn Comes.* New York: Holt, 1990. The beauty of the fall season in northern New England is displayed in this book. (Gr. 1-3)

McCully, Emily Arnold. *First Snow.* New York: Harper & Row, 1985. This wordless picture book about a mouse family's winter outing will generate conversation about winter activities. (Preschool-1)

Pearson, Susan. *My Favorite Time of Year.* Ill. by John Wallner. New York: Harper & Row, 1988. A family experiences the joys of each season as they watch the leaves turn, button up for winter, and spot the first robin. (Preschool-1)

Rockwell, Anne. *First Comes Spring.* New York: HarperCollins, 1991. Rockwell's family of bears stays busy throughout the year.(Preschool-1)

Rogers, Paul. *What Will the Weather Be Like Today?* New York: Greenwillow, 1990. Delightful illustrations and brief text make this a perfect book for early readers. (Preschool+)

Blackline Master 19

Today's Weather   Date _____

City	Temperature		Conditions
	°		Sunny ☀ Rain 🌧
_____	_____ °		
_____	_____ °		Cloudy ☁☁ Snow ❄
_____	_____ °		
_____	_____		Partly Cloudy

Visit a Flower Shop

Mistress Mary

Quite contrary;

How does your garden grow?

With silver bells

And cockleshells

And pretty maids all in a row.

Visit a local flower shop, the floral department in a grocery store, or walk around the neighborhood to look at flowers. Talk about the differences in the varieties and shapes, and have children identify the colors. Discuss with children why people like to have flowers in their homes and in their gardens. Talk about occasions when people send flowers to one another. If possible, have a floral worker demonstrate how a floral display is made and tell how the flowers are shipped from countries such as Mexico to flower markets in the United States. Discuss the roles of workers and customers at a floral shop. Demonstrate how orders for flowers are taken on the telephone. Model conversations florists might have with customers regarding costs of the bouquets, flower and color choices, and where the arrangements or plants should be sent. As you do, use a copy of the *Flower Order Form* (Blackline Master 20), showing children how it might be filled in.

flower, plant, florist, bouquet, celebrate, party, happy, beautiful, greeting cards, colors, customer, pot, soil, seeds, watering, sunlight

- Use topically related books, such as those in the list that follows, in introducing the center and during its use. Book-related activities should include reading aloud to children and opportunities for them to explore the books on their own.
- Provide seed and bulb catalogs, flower seed packets, and flower books.
- Encourage children to plant seeds in individual containers, to care for the plants, and to log the plants' growth in observation journals.
- Place home gardening and plant care books in the center.
- Invite children to make a flower collage using catalog pictures.
- Provide brochures showing floral bouquets and arrangements that are available at local floral shops.
- Encourage children to do a survey of favorite colors of flowers and then make charts recording those colors.
- After looking at catalogs, have children list the names of favorite flowers on a chart and illustrate each one. Display the chart in the shop so that customers can refer to the chart when ordering.
- Have children brainstorm materials they can use to make flowers, such as pasting torn paper petals on background paper. Demonstrate how to make petals curl by wrapping them around a pencil.
- Invite children to paint large flowers at the easels.
- Show samples of greeting cards that are attached to bouquets and then have children make their own.
- Invite parents to send in cuttings and flowers from their own gardens.
- Show children how to make dried flowers.
- Provide Blackline Master 20, *Flower Order Form* and *Greeting Cards*. Encourage children to use these forms in the center as they practice their writing (real or invented).

shelves for display	cash register	telephone
plants	pots for planting	soil
seeds	trowel	watering can

telephone book	seed and bulb catalogs	flower seed packets
greeting cards	paper, pencils	plant care and gardening books
brochures from florists	flower charts	flower shop posters
construction paper	Blackline Master 20, *Flower Order Form, Greeting Cards*	

BOOKS TO READ

Cooney, Barbara. *Miss Rumphius*. New York: Viking, 1982. A little girl promises her grandfather that someday, she will make the world more beautiful. When she is old, she accomplishes her mission by planting fields of lupines. (Kindergarten-3)

Demi. *The Empty Pot*. New York: Holt, 1990. The child who raises the best flower from a seed will become the new Emperor. The children do not know that the seeds they have been given are cooked ones. (Preschool-2)

Ehlert, Lois. *Growing Vegetable Soup*. San Diego: Harcourt, 1987. Bright colors and bold graphics make this a vegetable garden to remember. (Preschool-3)

McMillan, Bruce. *Counting Wildflowers*. New York: Lothrop, Lee & Shepard, 1986. The concepts of counting, colors, and flowers are reinforced by vibrant photographs. (Preschool-1)

_____. *Growing Colors*. New York: Lothrop, Lee & Shepard, 1988. Viewers will enjoy identifying colors as they look at photographs of fruits and vegetables. (Preschool-2)

Provensen, Alice and Martin. *The Year at Maple Hill Farm*. New York: Atheneum, 1981. Readers will discover interesting facts about farms and farm animals as the seasons progress in this well-loved picture book. (Preschool-2)

Rockwell, Anne. *Apples and Pumpkins*. Ill. by Lizzy Rockwell. New York: Macmillan, 1989. The apples and pumpkins picked on the farm become jack-o-lanterns and treats at Halloween. (Preschool-1)

Blackline Master 20

Flower Order Form

Name _____

Date _____

I want _____

_____

Deliver:

Monday	☐	Wednesday	☐	Friday	☐	Sunday	☐
Tuesday	☐	Thursday	☐	Saturday	☐		

To:

From:

Have a Good Day!

From:

Happy Birthday!

From:

Let's Go Camping

Remember when you and your best friend made a tent out of a blanket in your backyard? You brought a flashlight, a little bit of food, a pillow, and your favorite stuffed animals. Your pretend camping trip in the woods, away from adults, was spooky, and scary, and wonderful. Those pretend trips still are.

Model Language

Invite children to share any camping experiences they have had and to talk about why people like to go camping. Read *Bailey Goes Camping* by Kevin Henkes (Greenwillow, 1985). Have children pantomime actions as you describe camping activities. Wake up in the tent, stretch and yawn, warm yourself up, unzip your sleeping bag and the tent zipper, start the fire, get water, and so on. Show children camping equipment such as a sleeping bag, flashlight, canteen or water carrier. Encourage children to think about camping activities and to compare them to activities done at home. How is sleeping in a tent different than sleeping in a room? What would be different about cooking out-of-doors and cooking in a kitchen? How about brushing your teeth? Have children decide what area of the room would be most suitable for a camp site and then have them make suggestions about equipment that is needed. Have children create a list of the equipment, supplies, and food needed for a camping trip. Use the forms on Blackline Master 21 in your class planning.

Related Vocabulary & Concepts

camping, campgrounds, tent, woods, campfire, flashlight, sleeping bag, nature, singing, roasting/toasting, canteen/water carrier, nighttime, home, trip

- Provide state or national park brochures that show pictures and maps of camping areas and sites. Encourage children to discuss where they might like to camp, such as wooded, beach, or mountain areas.
- Provide a small tent or hang a sheet or a blanket over a rope strung across a corner of the room. Secure the corners of the blanket with rocks or blocks.
- Encourage children to establish rules for the use of the center, such as having only two in the tent at the same time. Have children write and post the rules at the camp site.
- Invite children to think of a name for the camp ground and make identifying signs and other labels, such as *Firewood Sold Here, Water,* or *Snack Shop.*
- Make a camp fire by wrapping rolled newspapers in brown construction paper. Add crumpled red and orange paper to represent burning coals. Place a lighted flashlight in the center of the fire. Make a fire ring using rocks.
- Encourage campers to sing familiar songs around the campfire.
- Encourage children to use utensils and dishes from the housekeeping center to pretend cook meals as they camp.
- Encourage campers to read books and magazines inside and outside the tent.
- Demonstrate writing in a camping journal, logging the animals observed, and meals cooked.
- Invite a boy scout or a girl scout to talk about camping experiences and equipment.
- Provide Blackline Master 21, *Camping Checklist* and *Meal Planner.* Remind children how you used these forms together in planning the center, and encourage them to make new ones as they continue their play.

tent—sheet or blanket	sleeping bags or mats	canteen or other water carrier
flashlight	eating utensils	empty container for insect repellent
empty food containers	pots and pans	small cooler
pretend camp fire		

Literacy Materials

travel brochures	pencils	state and national parks brochures
campground signs	journals for observations	directional signs and labels
campsite maps	books and magazines	binoculars
Blackline Master 21, *Camping Checklist, Meal Planner*		

OOKS TO READ

Arnosky, Jim. *In the Forest.* New York: Lothrop, Lee & Shepard, 1989. The artist's sensitive paintings and text describe different settings in the forest. (Gr. 2-4)

_____ . *Otters Under Water.* New York: Putnam, 1992. Beautiful illustrations gently show the antics and activities of otter pups and their mother. As with all of the author's books, this one gives wonderful insights of animal life. (Preschool-2)

Henkes, Kevin. *Bailey Goes Camping.* New York: Greenwillow, 1985. A bunny who cannot go to camp with his older siblings is taken on an imaginary camping trip with his parents. A delightful book. (Preschool-1)

MacDonald, Amy. *Little Beaver and the Echo.* Ill. by Sarah Fox-Davies. New York: Putnam, 1990. Would-be campers should know what the lonely little beaver in this story learns—that an echo can be a friend. (Kindergarten-2)

McPhail, David. *Pig Pig Goes to Camp.* New York: Dutton, 1983. The loveable pig loves camp! (Preschool-3)

Tejima, Keizaburo. *The Bears' Autumn.* LaJolla, CA: Green Tiger Press, 1986. Campers need to know about bears. This bear story tells about a baby bear's first fishing expedition with its mother. (Kindergarten-3)

Blackline Master 21

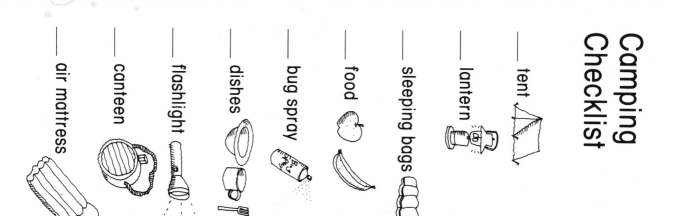

Camping Checklist

— tent

— lantern

— sleeping bags

— food

— bug spray

— dishes

— flashlight

— canteen

— air mattress

✂ -

Meal Planner	Monday	Tuesday
Wednesday	Thursday	Friday
Saturday	Sunday	

Create An Insect Museum

Bugs. Children love them. Their fascination with insects can generate lots of research, observation, and scientific journaling. Because of the size relationship, the insect world makes children feel big and powerful. Celebrate bugs!

Engage children in a discussion about insects they have seen, encouraging them to name and describe them. How large or small were they? How did they move? What colors were they? Write *entomologist* on the board, explaining that the word describes a scientist who studies insects. Tell children that there are many, many different types of insects to know about, and that people find insects so interesting that they often include displays of them in museums. Invite children to talk about experiences they have had visiting natural history, trail-side museums, or nature centers where insects are displayed. Before setting up a museum, invite children to go on an insect search so that they can observe real insects before creating pretend ones. Provide books that show illustrations of insects, such as *Bugs* by Nancy Winslow Parker and Joan Richards Wright (Greenwillow, 1987). Talk about the similarities and differences between various insects and how they differ from spiders. Invite children to brainstorm what could be included in a classroom insect museum.

insect, arachnid, spider, antennae, wings, thorax, museum, guide, observation, habitat, big/small, magnifying glass

- Provide picture books about insects and spiders (arachnids) to be placed in the center.
- Encourage children to draw varieties of insects, labeling their drawings with insect names.
- Have children cut out and mount their insects on paper for display.
- Invite children to make beetles and larger varieties of insects using playdough.
- Provide magnifying glasses.
- Encourage children to make insect cages or habitats for live insects using empty cardboard cartons. Have children decide what insects need to live, such as water, leaves, twigs, and grasses.
- Provide a notebook in which children can record observations of insects.
- Place child-made paper insects in cardboard box habitats.
- Encourage children to create fact sheets about various insects for museum visitors, illustrating their writings.
- Encourage children to create a museum entrance and registration desk where visitors can register and tickets can be sold.
- Invite children to make signs, such as *Museum Open 9:00 - 5:00, Feeding Time: 10:30, Big Insects* and *Little Insects*.
- Have children take turns being museum tour guides, pointing out interesting features and insects to visitors.
- Provide Blackline Master 22, *Insect Detective Sheet* and *My Best Bug*. Take children on a walk in your schoolyard or neighborhood—they are detectives, looking for as many bugs as they can possibly see. Encourage them to examine their finds carefully. Once back in the classroom, distribute copies of the Blackline Master. Ask children to complete the forms. (Those needing help can dictate their responses.) Provide time for sharing.

table and chairs	shelves for display	cardboard boxes
magnifying boxes	playdough	tweezers for moving paper insects

museum tickets   notebook for recording observations

insect labels   picture books and insect reference books

museum signs   paper and writing/drawing materials

Blackline Master 22, *Insect Detective Sheet*, *My Best Bug*

BOOKS TO READ

Brown, Ruth. *Ladybug, Ladybug*. New York: Dutton, 1988. In this book, beautiful illustrations accompany the familiar rhyme. (Preschool-1)

Carle, Eric. *The Very Quiet Cricket: A Multi-Sensory Book*. New York: Philomel, 1990. Readers will be delighted with the surprise ending in this book about a cricket who cannot chirp. (Preschool-1)

_____. *The Very Busy Spider*. New York: Philomel, 1989. A spider completes spinning a web while farm animals try to entice it to play. A repetitive, predictable book that invites shared reading. (Preschool-2)

Graham, Margaret Bloy. *Be Nice to Spiders*. New York: Harper & Row, 1967. In this amusing story, Helen the spider makes a fly-ridden zoo a peaceful place once again. (Kindergarten-3)

Maxner, Joyce. *Nicholas Cricket*. Ill. by William Joyce. New York: Harper & Row, 1989. In this fantasy, Nicholas and his Bug-a-Wug Cricket Band celebrate summer evenings as they play tunes for other insect party-goers. (Kindergarten-3)

Parker, Nancy Winslow and Wright, Joan Richards. *Bugs*. New York: Greenwillow, 1987. Readers will receive clear and concise information about insects in this cleverly written book. (Gr. 1-4)

Selsam, Millicent E. *Backyard Insects*. Photographs by Ronald Goor. New York: Scholastic, 1988. The interesting photographs in this book invite close observation of insects. (Preschool-3)

Van Allsburg, Chris. *Two Bad Ants*. Boston: Houghton Mifflin, 1988. A trip to a sugar bowl is the beginning of a harrowing adventure for two ants. (Preschool+)

Blackline Master 22

Insect Detective's Name _____

Name of Bug _____

This is what the bug looks like:

```
┌──────────────────────────────────────────────────┐
│                                                    │
│                                                    │
│                                                    │
│                                                    │
│                                                    │
│                                                    │
│                                                    │
│                                                    │
│                                                    │
└──────────────────────────────────────────────────┘
```

- - ✂ -

My Best Bug

Name _____

My favorite bug is _____

because _____

Run a
Bee Keeping
Station

I'm bringing home a baby bumblebee,

Won't my mommy be so proud of me!

I'm bringing home a baby bumblebee:

Buzz, buzz, buzz! Whoops! It stung me!

Honey

Honey is sweet
oney tastes good
es collect
pollen
make honey

Look at the pictures in books, such as *The Life Cycle of a Bee by Jill Bailey* (Watts, 1990), *The Honeybee in the Meadow* by Christopher O'Toole (Gareth Stevens, 1989), or *A Day in the Life of a Beekeeper* by Penny Michels and Judith Tropea (Troll Associates, 1991) so that children have a beginning understanding of bees and honey-making. Invite children to talk about experiences they have had with bees or bee stings. Talk about the reasons that we need bees in the world to pollinate flowers and fruit trees. Talk about the types of bees, such as queen, drone, or worker, and the jobs they do. Provide honey so that children can taste it, perhaps on crackers. Tell them that honey is used as an ingredient in recipes. Encourage children to describe the taste of honey, comparing it with other foods. Brainstorm with children what equipment should be included in a bee keeping station, such as hives, clothing for the keepers, pretend bees, honey-collecting equipment, and record keeping materials.

bees, wasps, pollinate, hive, comb, clover, bee keeper, queen, worker, dancing, flowers, yellow, black

- Invite children to make bees for the center using yellow cotton balls and attaching black construction paper or cloth wings and eyes. Make stripes using black pipe cleaners. Cotton balls can be colored by placing them in a small paper bag together with a small amount of dry tempera paint. Let children take turns shaking the bag.
- Create hives by painting shirt or dress boxes and stacking them vertically. Let children number the hives.
- Discuss protective clothing. Provide brimmed hats with netting attached, smocks, and gloves for the beekeepers.
- Provide empty containers in which children can pretend to collect and pour honey.
- Have children create charts on which they can record how much honey has been collected.
- Encourage children to make drawings of worker, drones, and queen bees, labeling and displaying their drawings in the center.
- Invite children to make honeycombs using egg cartons or by drawing comblike structures on paper.
- Make a honey snack shop next to the bee-keeping area so that children can serve honey and crackers.
- Have children make signs for the center. Decorate the snack shop with paintings of bees and flowers.
- Write recipes using honey as an ingredient on chart paper. Encourage children to copy the recipe to take home.
- Provide plastic squeeze bottles for the honey.
- Use Blackline Master 23, *Bee Keeping Record*. Provide time for children to share their completed worksheets with the class.

table and chairs	empty plastic containers	shirt or dress boxes
smocks	hats with netting	magnifying glasses
gloves	egg cartons	honey, crackers

drawings/labels of bees	picture and reference books	charts for recording
recipe charts	pads of paper and pencils for record keeping and observation	
honey snack shop signs	Blackline Master 23, *Bee Keeping Record*	

BOOKS TO READ

■ Bailey, Jill. *The Life Cycle of a Bee.* New York: Watts, 1990. Clear explanations and good illustrations make this book an excellent resource. (Preschool-3)

■ Michels, Penny, and Tropea, Judith. *A Day in the Life of a Beekeeper.* Photographs by John Halpern. New York: Troll Associates, 1990. This photo-essay provides an up-close look at a colony of bees and describes how they make honey. (Gr. 4+)

■ O'Toole, Christopher. *Discovering Bees and Wasps.* New York: Watts, 1986. The information in this book can be used as a resource for teachers while children will enjoy the photographs. (Gr. K-6)

Blackline Master 23

Bee Keeping Record

I have _____ bees.

I have _____ jars of honey.

My Bees

Explore an Underground Cave

Crawling into dark places, exploring under furniture, and sitting in private spaces is just a little bit scary and oh, so adventuresome. You never know what you will find in a classroom cave. Certainly you'll find rock collectors and samples of interesting rocks. Think of the rock collections that might be started!

Take an imaginary trip into a cave. Invite children to close their eyes as you describe putting on your non-slip shoes, walking down a path or climbing down a rope, crawling and sliding through the cave as it becomes darker and darker. Turn on your high-powered flashlight and describe what you see: pools of black water, giant worms, huge snails, and friendly snakes. Encourage children to take turns telling what they see on their underground cave trips. Have children tell why they think exploring caves would be adventurous. Then invite children to brainstorm what they need to do to create a cave in the classroom. Read Michael Rosen's *We're Going on a Bear Hunt* (Macmillan, 1989) to discover a bear in a cave. Provide pictures of caves so that children can see underground rock formations.

cave, spelunker, dark, rocks, stalactite, stalagmite, worms, snakes, bats, safety, light, entrance.

- Establish the cave under a table. Drape a sheet or blanket over the table. Or, provide a large appliance box in which the cave can be created. Movable room partitions can also be used to make the walls of the cave; use a sheet as a cave ceiling.
- Invite children to paint the walls of the cave on large sheets of newsprint paper.
- Children might enjoy making construction paper bats and attaching them with string to the roof of the cave.
- Encourage children to make construction paper, cardboard tube, or modeling clay snails, worms, and other underground creatures.
- Place large rocks in the cave.
- Provide small rocks for children to collect and bring out of the cave. Have children classify the rocks by color, size, or material.
- Invite children to establish safety rules for the cave, such as limiting the number of people, using soft voices, and setting a time limit for each exploratory team.
- Discuss with children appropriate activities for the cave, such as keeping a record of animal life seen, writing a description of the trip, or referring to cave maps and guides or reference books. In your discussion, show children how the forms on Blackline Master 24 could be used.
- List the names of existing caves, such as Carlsbad, Jewel, Wind, or Mammoth. Have children name their cave and display a sign over the entrance.
- Have children write a list of safety rules for explorers.
- Establish a sign-in and timing station at the cave entrance.
- Provide notebooks and pencils so that children can log their experiences inside the cave.
- Include in the center copies of books, fiction and nonfiction, about the creatures that might be found in a cave.
- Provide Blackline Master 24, *Cave Map* and *Creature Observation Data*. Remind children why a map and record would be important to real spelunkers. Encourage children to make their own maps and keep their own records as they use the center. Provide time for sharing.

sign-in table and chairs	cave walls	sheet or blanket
newsprint paper	construction paper	paints
modeling clay	flashlights	climbing ropes
boots	gloves	hard hat
rocks	small rocks for classifying	pouches for rocks

sign-in register	*We're Going on a Bear Hunt* by Michael Rosen (Macmillan, 1989)	
timing chart	notebooks for journaling	picture and reference books
cave maps	chart of cave rules	paper for listing observations

sheets for recording rock classifications

Blackline Master 24, *My Cave Map, Creation Observation Data*

BOOKS TO READ

Barrett, Norman. *Snakes.* New York: Watts, 1989. This volume is appropriate for the science table so that children can look at the photographs of various kinds of snakes. (Gr. 1-6)

Carle, Eric. *The Mixed-Up Chameleon.* 2nd edition. New York: Crowell, 1984. The poor chameleon, who is unhappy with the way he looks, tries out various colors. (Preschool-3)

Henwood, Chris. *Earthworms.* New York: Watts, 1988. Readers will not only learn interesting facts about earthworms, they will learn how to keep them for observation. (Gr. 1-3)

Lauber, Patricia. *Snakes Are Hunters.* New York: Crowell, 1988. Portions of this book can be read aloud if children are interested in the snake kingdom. (Kindergarten-3)

Lionni, Leo. *Inch by Inch.* New York: Astor-Honor, 1962. Lionni's classic collages accompany this tale of an inch worm that avoids being eaten by birds. (Preschool-2)

_____. *The Biggest House in the World.* New York: Pantheon, 1968. A little snail learns that having a shell as big as a birthday cake is not desirable.(Kindergarten-3)

Ryder, Joanne. *The Snail's Spell.* Ill. by Lynn Cherry. New York: Puffin, 1988. After reading this book, children will enjoy creative movement activities. (Gr. 2-4)

My Cave Map

- - ✄ -

Creature Observation Data

Bug's Name _____   *How many?* _____

What are the bugs doing? _____

_____

DATE DUE

MAR 2 8 1995	
OCT 1 6 1995	
SEP 2 8 1997	
NOV 1 0 1998	
MAR 0 8 1999	
NOV 1 0 1999	
NOV 2 8 1999	
OCT 0 7 2000	
FEB 1 4 2002	
DEC 1 3 2002	
MAY 0 6 2005	
WITHDRAWN	